Accidental Origami
new and selected poems

Accidental Origami
new and selected poems

by karla k. morton

Texas Review Press
Huntsville, Texas

FIRST EDITION
Requests for permission to acknowledge material from the work should be sent to:

> Permissions
> Texas Review Press
> English Department
> Sam Houston State University
> Huntsville, TX 77341-2146

ACKNOWLEDGMENTS:
"For Love and Michelangelo" first appeared in *Concho Review;* "On the Way to Santa Fe" first appeared in the *Mojave Review;* "Hanging On" first appeared in *AmarilloBay;* "Superman's Birthday" first appeared in *descant;* "Woman in the Pipe Shop" first appeared in *Southwestern American Literature;* "Becoming Superman" first appeared in *ARDENT Journal;* "Ask the Crow" first appeared in *ARDENT Journal;* "Charmer" first appeared in *descant;* "What Goes Unseen" first appeared in *borderlands;* "Statistics" first appeared in *Wise Ass Journal;* "Redefining Beauty" first appeared in *REAL: Regarding Arts and Literature Journal;* "A Rare Man" first appeared in *di-ver-si-ty journal;* "Snakes" first appeared in *Southwestern American Literature;* "Standing by the Bok Choy, Central Market, Plano Texas" first appeared in *Wichita Falls Literary and Art Review;* "You Don't Know Hot" first appeared in *Texas Poetry Calendar;* "Where Moonlight Cannot Tread" first appeared in *Denton Writers' League Anthology;* "Crybaby" first appeared in *Austin International Poetry Anthology;* "Passing the Gauntlet" first appeared in *descant;* "Paris as I See It" first appeared in *Cooking with the Texas Poets Laureate;* "Anniversary" first appeared in *Southwestern American Literature;* "Horseshoes" first appeared in *Southwestern American Literature;* "When Texas No Longer Fits in the Glove Box" first appeared in *Texas Poetry Calendar;* "Cowboys We Are" first appeared in *Cowboy Poetry Press*

Cover photo by karla k. morton
Cover design courtesy of Nancy Parsons

Library of Congress Cataloging-in-Publication Data

Names: Morton, Karla K., author.
Title: Accidental origami : new and selected works / karla k. morton.
Description: Edition: first. | Huntsville, Texas : Texas Review Press, 2016.
  | Contains selections from the author's previous 10 poetry anthologies, as
  well as new material.
Identifiers: LCCN 2015047511 (print) | LCCN 2015048375 (ebook) | ISBN
  9781680030877 (pbk. : alk. paper) | ISBN 9781680030884 (e-book)
Classification: LCC PS3613.O77864 A6 2016 (print) | LCC PS3613.O77864 (ebook)
  | DDC 811/.6--dc23
LC record available at http://lccn.loc.gov/2015047511

*To my fifth grade teacher, Mrs. Aaron
of Maxie Speer Elementary
in Arlington, Texas,
and to all Teachers everywhere
who hold the power to change the world
one student at a time.*

Contents

New Works

1   Aperçu
2   On the Way to Santa Fe
3   To a Pregnant Daughter
4   One Summer of Eighteen
5   321
6   Symmetry
8   Statistics
10   Amateur Numerology
12   Bed Head
13   A Night in Tyler
14   Evolution
16   Hate Bus
17   One Song
18   A Man's World
19   Global Warming
20   Sympathy for Prometheus
21   Ambition
22   For you,
23   Echo
24   Ashes
25   What We Do
26   Life and Death in the Cotton Fields
27   Who Gives This Person?
28   When Bonnie Found Clyde
29   Love Song of Bonnie Parker
30   Grey Area on Dove Road
31   The Warrior
32   Time
33   Music
34   Lift of Dreams
35   When God Speaks
36   Alphitomancy
37   Cowboys We Are
38   Ventifacts
39   Asclepius
40   Mending
42   The Importance of Coffee

TCU Texas Poets Laureate Series

(TCU Press)

45 Alamo Coastline
46 For Love and Michelangelo
47 Bursting into Snowflakes
48 Electronic Quills
49 Graveside in Sanger
50 Bad Theology
51 Indian Blood
52 Where Moonlight Cannot Tread
54 Superman's Birthday
55 Shattering the Ordinary
56 When Texas No Longer Fits in the Glove Box
58 The Closer
60 Hanging On
61 The Monarch and Her Mistress
62 Living Close to DFW Airport, September 12, 2001
63 Woman in the Pipe Shop
64 Picking Up the Accent

Redefining Beauty

(Dos Gatos Press)

69 Honeysuckle
70 Spock Thinks I'm Sexy
71 Second Spring
72 Cowboyed Up
73 Redefining Beauty

Wee Cowrin' Timorous Beastie

(a 17th-Century Scottish Epic CD and Book by Lagniappe Publishing)

77 Wee Cowrin' Timorous Beastie

Becoming Superman

(Zone Press)

91 Becoming Superman
92 Don't Be Nervous
93 Teenage, Burning
94 Texas Longhorns
95 Ask the Crow

Names We've Never Known
(Texas Review Press)

99   Charmer
100 Atheists
101 What Goes Unseen
102 Snakes
103 Summer at Texoma
104 Directionally Impaired
105 Texas Heirlooms
106 What Really Makes the Stars Shine
107 Standing by the Bok Choy, Central Market, Plano Texas
108 A Rare Man
109 Austin Embrace
110 Superconductivity
111 Ultimate Sacrifice
112 An Ordinary Moment of Extraordinary Beauty
     on Northside Drive
113 Alvarado Coy
114 Crybaby
115 In Your Prime
116 The Old That's Worth Hanging On To
118 Horseshoes
119 Anniversary

Stirring Goldfish
(Finishing Line Press)

123 Circles
124 Wishes
125 River and Snake
126 Redefining Strength
127 Deep Sleep
128 Silence
129 Royal Purple
130 Lifting Up
131 Faith
132 Rush
133 Ready
134 Hope
135 Joy
136 Peace
137 Wanting
138 Returning

Hometown, Texas:

Young Poets & Artists Celebrate Their Roots

(TCU Press)

141 Leaving Brenham
142 Traveling with Dog
143 Making Peace with Scorpions
144 Bowie Snow Globes
145 Danny Keough
146 Calling the Cattle

Passion, Art, Community:

Denton, Texas, in Word and Image

(The City of Denton, Texas)

151 Fun
152 The Last Raid, 1874
153 Capital Punishment
154 Hickory Creek
156 New Icaria
158 An Old Photo of Young Men
159 May Comes to Denton County
160 Small Town Bees: a poet's thank you to Denton, Texas

8 Voices:

Contemporary Poetry of the American Southwest

(Baskerville Publishers)

165 Palindrome
166 The E Ticket
167 Tree Blossoms
168 Persephone, the Bear
170 Motel
171 Sign Language
172 One Night in Florida

Constant State of Leaping

(The Texas Review Press)

175 Weeding
176 A Perfect Night at the Observatory,
177 What Real Men Do
178 Adytum
179 You Don't Know Hot

180 Winter
181 Letter to the Grim Reaper
182 The Making of a Hero
183 Passing the Gauntlet
184 Walking Out
185 Midnight on the Roof at Villa Velleron
186 Breathless
187 Good Saturday
188 Contemplating the Nut
189 Whisper in the Winter
190 Letter to an Old Love
191 The Eternal Life of Poets
192 Tiny Courtships
193 Tequila Poetry Form
    (2-2-4-3)
194 Sin
195 Seasons
196 God Bless America
197 God in the Bathtub
198 Twelve Stitches
199 Reference Material
200 Shameless Love Poem
201 My Moment of America
202 veronica
204 Her Night Eyes
205 A Little Flower

Cooking with the Texas Poets Laureate

(Texas Review Press)

209 Jell-O Healing
210 Paris as I See It
211 Damn Dishes
212 What Clings to the Back of the Spoon
213 Music Box Lunch

New Works

Aperçu*

You ask me to sum up this manuscript
in 90 seconds—
a ride in an elevator,
200 words or less.

But this is a book of *poems*—
those things lodged in the heart
brought on by bacon and chocolate
and war and kids that miss their curfew
and sisters dying
and a kiss that punctures façade.

And they're for *you*—to roll in,
to swallow, to seep in your bloodstream
and pound open the chamber doors
of your own heart.

They are interior dwellers—
those things that rise in your chest;
that suffer the back of your throat till you
speak their name.

They are memory and breath and need.
They are the 88 spring times we wish
we could have;
the lush grape before the wine,
the stained lips after.

---

*aperçu—a glimpse, insight, or summary

On the Way to Santa Fe

for Beth Patterson and Melanie Watson

We stopped to picnic along the Palo Duro rim
with cheese and olives and almond crackers
and a flight of champagne
to watch the sun slip down.

But night didn't fall like a closing curtain;
it rose—a cool, purple breath
from the canyon floor;
up, from the shadow of spiked bush,
up from the holes of masked coons,
like the slow howl of coyote;
up like the wafting musk of all beasted things
overflowing the canyon into the air,
until we were *all* the colour of night.

It is not the light, but the dark
where all things begin—
our pupils wide and wild;
once more the carnivores of gnashing molars
and long eye tooth;

hair bursting from our legs;
the bottles, the cooler, the truck
lost like overgrown civilization;
our bodies reverting to scavenge and smell
and scrape of nail.

How odd to be so empowered
by only earth and water and air;
our worn wombs clinging to the scattered afterbirth
of creation.

We who bring life into the world, still feel it—
the slow, twisting grasp of evolution:
the darkness;
the ancient sparks
like the tumbling, trembling stars.

To a Pregnant Daughter

In you, my child,
is the voice of your grandmother,
and her grandmother,
and her grandmother before her—
all the way back to the first anxious mother,
when Eve sang to Cain
in the caves beyond Eden.

There was music from the beginning,
the sweet wielding of inflection;
a humming of suckling and swaddling;
a rocking side to side, notes rising
through pacing feet
hush little baby, don't say a word
up, rising up;
lullaby passed through
blood and milk and restless nights.

Do not worry.
Your hips know how to push
and balance and sway;
your hands know fever and temper;
your eyes know danger.

Your ears, so close to the throat,
know hunger and need—
and the lips respond
from some dark memory.

Time is infinite in the feminine—
a swirl of struggle and pleasure;
your voice, already fruited;
ripe with ancient song.

One Summer of Eighteen

One more day at the lake
before the excitement
of packing for college—
a new chapter for us all;

the Sun, soft in farewells, dropping
to the water—an orange silk rug
to lead us to shore.
The kids, spent, after hours

of heat and swimming,
draped over each other in naps,
like puppies.
Do they know there's only

one summer of eighteen?
childhood swinging behind them
in their rush; slammed shut
like the thin screen door.

321

Room Number Poetry Form

There is blood
on the sheets.
Housekeeping
will think me
a virgin.
There is blood
on the sheets.

Indeed
tonight
with you

I
was.

Symmetry

Ours is a God fond of symmetry—
day and night,
tree and root;
sky and sea;
the world reckoned
as two hinge upon each other.

I like the long pleats
of your khakis;
the way those Wranglers curve
around your gluts;
the way nothing ever fits your arms—
sleeves shrunken from their long trip
over muscle and forearm,
cuffs turned up,
then up again.

I like the way your mountain hat
balances your height;
the way a suit
squares your gladiator shoulders
like armor.

Ours is a God fond of symmetry;
the way you have one of that
and two of those;
the way I have two of these
and one of this;

the way my cheek fits
in the soft bowl of your palm;
the way our destinies merge—
as smooth in purpose
as a button into cloth.

I am here.
You are there.
You are night and sea and root.

And at dusk, on the four corners of His throne,
God smiles at the way
day gives itself to night,

the rim of thin lips
between the sea and the sky,
and the way the roots, never once,
abandon their depth—
never forsaking the weight of the tree;
the bounty, the bark, the blossom.

Statistics

1 out of 2 psychologists
suggested I write this letter to you—
dear husband, and your friends.

I must tell you,
I am, as 50% of married couples,
divorcing *all* of you.

1 out of 6 people get cancer,
and not once have you *ever* thanked me.
I'm tired of being your bald fall guy.

Besides, at least once a year,
1 out of 8 billion people on earth
has chided you for being so mean,
so I know this isn't in my head—
it's not even in the CAT scans that catch
7 out of 10 mental ailments.

100% of my heart agrees.
I'm tired of this,
and I'm tired of all of *you*,
with your Botox foreheads
and fake boobs,
your cigarettes and meth
and lipo and prescription drugs;
your alcoholic state every night;
your years of sunbathing
with baby oil and iodine.

I ate organic food,
never tried nicotine,
refused face-lifting poisons,
passed on the heroin
and *excess* tequila shots . . .

yet here I am,
and not you.

Besides, 29% of all accidents
happen within 2–5 miles of home.

So, I'm out of here.
I'm taking my dog and my cat
and my computer;
my 1947 typewriter;
my black O'Keefe hat;
my record player and walking stick,
all my jewelry and books and boots.

I'm stopping at the liquor store
on the way out,
eating fried chicken twice a week;
taking up pipes and cigars
and loud music.

Don't call.
Don't *ever* visit.

I'll be staying up till 2 am every night,
sleeping past 10 every morning,
sporting pajamas through lunch.

Some days, I won't even pick up
my toothbrush,
just to piss off *you*,
and 3 out of 4 dentists,
with their spray tans, perfect teeth,
and their 2.5 un-spanked, rotten,
healthy children.

Amateur Numerology

It's not lost on me
that I'm staying
in room 205 in this hotel—
the same number
as my father's hospital room.

2 0 5
The number must mean *something*.

A few blocks away,
our old house still lingers
at 809 N. West Street,
though the named changed years ago.
Our old phone number
was CR4-6667.
I was 11 when I first
called myself a poet.
I was born on the 28th.
I have 2 children.
I always bet on 13.
I see the clock at 1:11 or 11:11.
I just turned 47.
I have 1 brother.
It is the 10th month.
My father, 81,
won't live to see November . . .

We both went to sleep in 205
last night,
my father and I.

But only I will rise in the morning
and pull on my boots,
and wonder about the magic
inside tiny synchronicities;

reaching for the solace of signs—
the number of gifts in each heart;
the number of heartbeats in each day;
the number of days in the life
of a good man.

Bed Head

I guess this isn't new to the curly-headed,
the way REMs gypsy out of the head every night
in the soft twirl of tambourines,
and shimmy the path of each hair
around and around the compass of follicle
till they're wild with direction.

Dreams of adventure shaking loose
their cluster of one another—
rebels every one
with their own hairy world to conquer.

This is the way with ambition,
that gut rock-and-roll
rising, jumping guard rails,
crossing borders.

A late night of strewn papers
and moonlit inspirations;
a village of ideas dancing on dusty bare feet;
the fall of sweet exhaustion into slumber.

Then comes the 2 am rousing;
the toss, the turns
long fingers loosening buttons,
sliding zippers,
the silver runes of tiny wristed bells.

A Night in Tyler

In the grand biography of my life,
it may not be noted
that I fell in love with Tyler,
that East Texas town
so proud of her roses;

that I spoke at the newly refurbished
Liberty Theater on the Square;
that I made deep friends;
that I spent a starry evening
in a Hilton by a field.

And in that night,
Skunk walked by my room,
raising his tufted tail in a greeting
that permeated locked windows,
and two rows of drapes.

And I smiled, remembering
s-shaped back roads
saturated in skunk;
days following old fence lines;
nights stretched on our backs,

the driveway concrete still warm,
naming planets as they popped up—
Venus, Jupiter, then Mars;
spying the Dipper's long handle,
its perfect cup of four stars.

Evolution

> *The only thing that separates us from the animals is our ability to accessorize.*
>
> —Robert Harling, *Steel Magnolias*

The line between the species must be growing thin.
My mother's dog mopes if his collar is off.
And there's a German Shepherd in Red River
that won't leave the laundry room
until his sweater is snug back on.
No raven can resist
the orphaned jewel on the ground.

In the evening, I pull off
my mane of necklaces, the stone bracers,
the silver weapons around my fingers,
and sink to the luxury of hot running water—
a meditation in cleanliness.

But there is nothing more human than the shave—
the slow ritual of razor running up the calf,
around the knee,
across thick muscle of thigh.

Dolphins have no need of it.
Elephants wouldn't consider it.
Chimpanzees are puzzled.
Even crows have learned to resist the silver glisten
of exposed blades.

But by my bath,
there is candlelight and books of poetry,
and after a while,
the slow, tinny scrape
of razor along warm flesh.

And the eyes and fingers follow.
And the lines are worked
and reworked
until all that's left
is the smoothed skin;

the wilderness held back
one more night.

Hate Bus

If I could teach you one word on your journey, my friends,
my feminine comrades, it would be
NO.

Say it loud and firm when he wants to take you
and you don't want to be taken;

when he berates you before the wide eyes of your children;
when he says your opinion means nothing.

Do this the very first time, and glint your eyes,
and snarl your words.

Go ahead and put those hands on your hips—

elbows bowed out to make you look bigger,
as though you've come across a mountain lion in your path;

never mind if it's adrenaline and illusion;
do it anyway.
Strength follows imitation.

And if he hits you—*even once*—
pull out your suitcase
while your skin still burns,
knowing *Sorry*'s just a little song he will sing.

Don't wait until it happens again,
arrogance feeding his fist,
when anger has settled in the ruts
like an old bus on a muddy road;

when the getting out seems impossible;

when the more you push
just seems
to work the hate in deeper.

One Song

You ask if I will ever grow tired
of the same eyes, the same cheeks,
the same hand curled in mine.

There are many things I do not know—
like quantum physics,
the paths of shooting stars,
the language of elephants,
the next Vesuvius eruption,
the rise and fall of Earth's waters.

Man was not made to soothsay.

But this I *do* know—
the first time I saw you,
something smoothed across my skin
like dawn along the eyelid of darkness;
hunger rushed its desires
from my belly to my heart.

Still, when you turn to me
in the wee hours of the morning,
the world shakes and settles
as it should;

the woes of night
scatter like fleeing crows;

and in the fields,
the old Earth rises anew,
birds begin their one and only song,

and the sunflowers lift those ancient faces
to the very same sky—
the Sun, a golden goddess in their eyes.

A Man's World

In 1988, one hour and 50 years
south of Raleigh;
hams hung in the General Store;
farmers in overalls
took coffee at 5 a.m.

And there we were,
young whippersnappers moving in—
out-of-state license plates
and a Doberman Pinscher,

not believing there existed
such flawless country roads
with miles of tobacco farms
and perfect little houses
on streets with no signs,
or home mail delivery;

or that posting *No Smoking* signs
was political suicide;
or that they had just taken down
the county's welcome sign:
Home of the Grand Dragon of the KKK.

And just a few months later, that town,
that Rockwall-esque town,
began counting the days until we *heathens*
would leave—

not believing themselves
that a husband would let his wife
paint nude pictures,
or drive all the way to Raleigh to work,
or sleep in on Sunday;
or send her to the Grocery
to try and buy beer *like a man.*

Global Warming

I read that Greenland is warming, actually going *back*
to the temperature it was when Erik the Red first arrived
and conquered. But those Norsemen didn't stay, their last

documented event—Thorstein and Sigrid's wedding in 1424.
And then, the records stop, as the weather grew harsh,
and the Vikings retreated. It's said, one day, the whole planet

will change, Texas growing barren—the Chihuahuan Desert,
prancing north in tiny yelps and spiky collars. So, everyone
who migrated here to pillage our women and plunder our

barbecue, feel free to move on, to prowl for cooler pastures.
Go ahead. We'll be fine. We've *been* down to Big Bend;
learned the taste of cactus; how to tell time by

the constellations; seen bluebonnets fat as tumbleweeds;
watched buzzards spread 6-foot wings, holding court
in the Terlingua Cemetery. Those Vikings were no Texans.

For us, it's not about the *weather*, it's about the *land*.
And should our Hill Country bloom become ocotillo
and lechuguilla, we would love her no less. Down in the Bend,

scorpions walk the tooled labyrinth of my boots; horny toads
like my singing. I'll oil-rig that flagpole till it spears the Rio
Grande; that one Lone Star, the only comfort I need.

Sympathy for Prometheus

Saturday morning comes with a price.
Back from the fish market,
he yanks off sheets
like white butcher paper,
a slap of palm on pale flesh
as sharp as morning air;
forcefully turning her
over,
then over again;
a whisky-stenched critique
of quality, of firmness,
of age;
fingers pulling, yanking,
probing;
then the knife of entry, the fillet.

She ponders the odd name of *cleaning*;
the regeneration of the liver.
Then he's gone,
still hungry, agitated;
still trying to figure out
just what she's taken from him;
leaving her to the birds of prey—
splayed, unmoving,
open-eyed.

Ambition

I married my husband
because it was so damn sexy—

that upward consuming flash

like the potted cactus Dad had.
One glass of water each night
spawning an inch ascent each day.

I ate of those thorns,
drank the grape Kool-Aid of faith;
nothing to stop my burst through closed doors;

refusing to pray for rain
after the sight of African drought—
elephant bones in the dust.

Naivety strung
in candy beads around my neck;

but God always heeding my call—
crashing through bricks,
His glass pitcher always full;
brushing off the mortar as I prayed

Hurry, Please—my dreams!—

what He's heard every night;
what's blown thick
to the wick
of 50 years
of birthday candles.

For you,

Billy,
I am leaving your book
out on the side table of this cruise ship
as I fetch a drink—half beer, half tomato juice.

I can only imagine what joy it would bring
to see your own book chosen among the many
for a vacation.

I'm reading you, half naked
on the top deck,
with 360 degrees of blue horizon.

It would be discerning to think about
the depth of the ocean,
or rogue waves,
or the thousands of fanged creatures
in the darkness below,
or my surgery when I return.

So I hold onto your book
through high tide and welter,
through squall and summer rain;
poetry, a buoyant life raft
in my hands.

– for Billy Collins

Echo

There will come a time
when all that is left
are words.
Death feigns kindness to the mortal.

Every visit to the book store,
I rush to find more Oliver,
more Olds, more Heaney,
more Hirsch, and McDonald and Stafford;
more Kooser; more Kumin,

knowing the day will come
when there is nothing new—
when they can write no more;
their essence coveted; vanished.

Our bodies breach slow as old trees—
limb by limb fail in the mirror—
an absence of form;
no hand left to hold a pen.

To those I love,
my heart will always glide about you
like the circling hawk,

but take my books to the mountain,
shout my words into the valley,
I will always *always* answer back.

Ashes

Days like this,
I think about the little blue house
on the jetty—
the one we actually could afford.

Mentally owning it after one viewing,
I was already having coffee and pie
with back porch pelicans
and endless waves.

The sale declined, then again for odd reasons,
I was angry.
Why can't we have a little beauty,
a warm slice of paradise,
salty coffee every morning?

Three months later, it burned to the ground,
ashes swirling around total destruction—
except that one iron chair on the porch.

It was a gift of knowledge, you know.
There is no *why* in faith.

Three treatments till finished,
my chemo delayed yet another week,
and the old anger bullies—
half the summer lost already.

I put myself back in that Florida chair,
lift praises of relief for my beaten veins—
as delicate as stems of dandelion;
force rest upon my body.

I think of a cabin waiting in the mountain,
two porch rockers of Aspen;
the way my clothes smell like the fireplace;

the aphorisms in ashes,
the way they always have a story
to tell.

What We Do

The evening brings rest to all but the lovesick poet.
                    —Petrarch

And here we are—
slanted, arched,
prostrate like lovers;
pen in hand,
doing what we cannot help but do;
molten words roiled from magma to lava,
roused and tempered
from our souls.

We understand the water bird,
the squirrel, the ant, the eagle—
those who toil for survival;

but love is uncanny;
footless.

It does not rise in the East,
nor set in the West.
It does not lounge in warmth
at noon.

Here lies the evening struggle—
to name what cannot be named;
to grasp something ethereal;
to hold the grey beauty of fog
in our thin, mortal hands.

Life and Death in the Cotton Fields

Outside Odessa,
the secrets of space
sink in ten-mile footprints
of meteors,

time is cast out
in the spray.
In such stillness,
silence becomes its own song.

How can we stand in these
bountiful fields,
Night dropping her purple cloak
about our shoulders,

and *not* think of things
greater than ourselves—
of the huge reach of joy;
the finite distance of life

between these heavens;
bolls of cotton curving
in a galaxy of white stars
at our feet.

Who Gives This Person?

What do we think then
about the square jaw of death;
his two-buttoned jacket
and skinny black tie.

Perhaps he shows up smelling good;
freshly shaved,
offering the crook of his arm,
our escort through that first long night.

"Mind the stones," he'd say,
in thick Scottish cant,
whistling Sinatra,
tapping black patent leather
down dawn's long procession,

handing us over
like father of the bride,
the alluvial veil
finally lifted from our eyes.

When Bonnie Found Clyde

It's what drought can do to a man—
the drought of a father
with no childhood for his sons;

his family sleeping under a wagon;
his heart cracking in fields
once soft with green.

Poor begets poor
like desperation to thievery,
like thievery to prison—
horrors clogging the mind.

Man has always been his own undoing.

It's what drought can do to a man—
turning schoolboy to rattlesnake;
each dark hole, an abyss the soul falls into.

Bonnie must have been
a cool river winding into his world;
the attraction urgent—
the water, the heat,
twisting the ominous storm.

There was love there,
in the thin roots of their lives . . .
but the world was wrong,
the earth was poor,
and the barren thirsted.

It's what drought can do to a man.

Love Song of Bonnie Parker

I will be your Bonnie
if you will be my Clyde;
the two of us front-seated
in this hot, barren ride of life.

What did they *do* to you
behind those iron bars?
They left you with only yourself
to believe in,
but I am here.

No one should *ever* treat you that way,
and together we will make them all pay—
all of them.
The only thing we've got is each other,
and *this* day.

We know now—
we were not meant to grow old, you and I.
So let's take what we can,
let this world be damned;
and whatever may come,
I'll be by your side.

I'm your Bonnie, my love.
You can be my Clyde.

Grey Area on Dove Road

On our days of Bonnie and Clyde Days Festival,
let some of us dress up as Deputy Malcolm Davis,
or Texas Troopers Edward Wheeler (on his second day of duty)
and H.D. Murphy, killed on Dove Road,
guns still in their holsters as they approached
that infamous Ford.

Let some wear a wedding dress,
like Trooper Murphy's fiancée
at his funeral;
or don black lace over the eyes, like Widow Wheeler,
married less than two years.

There were victims amid the glamour—
nine murders of lawmen and other civilians.

How easy to look to the rebellion—
the fighting back of a boy abused in jail,
released a worsened criminal;
to a girl, in love with the bad boy.

Ours is a world worn from tragedy,
escaping to the Hollywood gloss.
Sometimes we need heroes common as dust
who fight the way we wish we could.

But sometimes we need to give voice
to the innocent
like Florence McPherson,
engaged to Deputy Davis,
who never married.

The Slavs believe doves carry souls up to heaven.
Imagine old Miss McPherson,
the daily doves outside each window;
the same mourning song
for a hundred years*.

---

*Miss McPherson of Grapevine was engaged to Deputy Malcolm Davis. She
never married, and died at 100 years old

The Warrior

for Ron Moore

He seems more god than Greek;
more Greek than American;
confidence raising his chin
as he looks over his party guests.

I see him in full armor
beside Poseidon's Temple,
watching returning war ships,
reading victory in their flags.

He has traveled this world,
yet returned,
a lover's green aventurine
for his wrist.

Aventurine—
the stone of Greek warriors
for luck and healing.

And when the century comes,
and time seizes travel from his legs,
he'll turn inward
down that spiral staircase of his soul
into the hypogeum*

for the new adventure—
where Socrates sits,
wine in hand,
wrestling wisdom for her pearls,

where death is but another country
yet to conquer.

---

hypogeum—an underground vault or burial chamber

Time

And where did the day go?
A late Sunday of mingling legs,

sermons of hawk and crow,
a choir of mockingbird.

Sitting outside,
legs still reaching for one another,
together;

just words.

The hours, dulcet and vaulting
like dog years.

These are the best unremarkable
days of our life,

when nothing happens
but the bloom of tiny wildflowers,
the kind you have to sink to your knees
to see.

Music

It was my second love,
though I could not give up my first.
That's how it is with good lovers—

they come into your life all Mozart and Romeo,
the desire on their tongue
equal to a thousand lives,
yet they promise it all in one.

These things I am grateful for:
octaves of letters
that loop and tumble from my pen;
the notes of Mandolin and French Horn
blown back into the world.

There was this day
at the amusement park,
when we jazzed Sir Duke,*

our riff, a duende catching fire to the onlookers,
the judges.

It was sex and it was hot and it was *good*
and we blistered and rolled because it was *ours*—
a heat and flare to die for.

That is a lover—
made of God and light and hurdling heart,
who still burns 30 years later with just a thought.

It's the drumbeat locketed around our necks;
what sings from old yellow envelopes;

the very life we dare to open
when we raise our eyes
to the stars.

---

*"Sir Duke" by Stevie Wonder

Lift of Dreams

We must have looked like fools,
huddled around that two-sided fireplace—
her first maiden flame;
holding our breath like the Wright Brothers,

the final Hail Mary that it would work—
that smoke would rise up and out,
not flood the cabin.
And we *were* fools,

sinking every last dime of our savings
into a remote cabin on the most perfect
piece of real estate God ever invented.
The rules were specific—

three short fires, for only an hour,
no more than three half-logs at a time
to cure a fireplace most said would never draw.
Curls began to lift and we clamoured outside,

shielded the sun with our hands, rekindling
the dead with whoops and cheers—
that grey smoke rising,
rising like a prayer.

When God Speaks

It was the roses that did it—
long, foot-long stems;
a pink so perfect I cried.

A gift, you know—
everything is a gift.

Innocence clipped and shipped
in full bloom
that we may know beauty;
know gratitude.

Passersby in the market
said they smelled them
before they saw them—
twelve perfect blooms;
guardian petals browned on the edges
hovering over inner sweetness.

When I found them,
I knew it would be okay—
the curing, the healing;
swaddling those pink promises
like a newborn babe;
words as old as Alpha.

A woman told me today
she found her dead husband's
unsent love letters
in a box of his old books;
origami revelations.
The signs are everywhere.

All I could think of
were those ballerina pink roses,
and a gentle-handed Fate
who refuses to speak of destiny
lest he rob us
the joy of our faith.

Alphitomancy

divination with grains of barley

My mother-in-law opened her eyes when she died.
Two days of unconsciousness,
then the wide open moment of death.

The last thing she did on this earth was bake.
She baked her sweet barley bread,
ate of it,
and died.

Revelation has many names,
many still unspoken.

I offer my bucket to the horses—
grains of oats and barley
to fill their bellies,
and widen their eyes

like the white mare I saw
driving to Springer,

standing alone on a hill
beside one lone cedar tree.
She stared over the highway,
beyond the next butte,

unmoving, angelic,
the wind her only stirring,

looking at something only she could see;
a divination comprehended
from blood and brain and rumination—

that same look you get
when a poem comes upon you;

a mix of sky and light and future;
unborn;
destined.

Cowboys We Are

Into the night, the steer fear the dawning
Skittish of the dark, they low and they bray
So we, before bed, hum through our yawning
These heavenly moments under star spray

Come sing the night song, come stoke the old fires
Drink makes us young and drink makes us liars
Girls make us bold, old dogs make us criers
But cowboys we are at the end of day

A little more padding under our bed
Coffee we drink now with sugar and cream
Callouses softened, our bellies, well fed
But time can't erase our open range dream

Come sing the night song, come stoke the old fires
Drink makes us young and drink makes us liars
Girls make us bold, old dogs make us criers
Cowboys we are at the end of the day

We might work in banks or a bar in town
Be plumbers or lawyers—cleaning what sours
Watching the clock as it makes its countdown
For long weekends here—these rich, sacred hours

Cities are charging each pasture and tree
The world is changing from trail to highway
But as long as man needs sky to be free
Horses we'll saddle to round up each stray

Come sing the night song, come stoke the old fires
Drink makes us young and drink makes us liars
Girls make us bold, old dogs make us criers
Cowboys we are at the end of the day

Ventifacts

(rocks shaped by the wind)

Where is Mr. Mortality when you need him—
that mythical man who traveled graveyard
to graveyard, re-carving old headstones?

I can only read a handful here—
a cemetery of forgotten names;
so many lives lost to time.

But it's an odd comfort knowing even rock
is re-shaped by the elements; knowing
whatever harsh edges man chips into the world,

the earth will prevail, the long tongue of the wind
whetting each headstone like hot prairie saltlicks—
white and thinning and squared.

Asclepius

Son of Apollo and the Greek God of Healing.
The genus name of milkweed.

He'd found a sand dollar in the reef,
thrilled, mask up,
running to show it off, but stopped,
realizing it was *alive*,
turning, rushing it back to its salty home,
not keeping it like most would;

like *I* would, I'm ashamed to say—
my house filled with found rocks and shells.

This child knew to give it back to the sea;
back to its obscure life of growing and feeding
and roaming the ocean floor.

Perhaps this child should be told
monarch butterflies are swiftly declining—
farmers finally figuring out a way
to chemically rid their fields of milkweed
to increase harvest production—

milkweed, the main diet of migrating monarchs.

We turn to technology to try to cure Earth's ills—
trying to reverse global warming, and feed the world,
but it's the silence where all things are healed.

Life is lived in the immeasurable—
the marveled child;
the tacit weed beneath the corn.

Mending

The world is tethered,
strung too tight for too long,
coiling the only way it knows—
wild riot, chaos, mob;
looting neighbour's stores
for vodka and cell phones;

knots like this bobbin,
spinning wrong;
winding worse with each half hour;

God straining to hear
through screaming, torched police cars,
spewing cans of tear gas.

I stop for a moment
to listen to the night,
the soft nicker of the horses;
the pull and munch of grass.

Somewhere in Ferguson, Missouri,
New York, LA, and Dallas,
grass grows just like this,
offering up its gentle hands.

Slowly I unwind
and wind again the bobbin,
ease the grey thread
into the slim steel eyes.

All the colours of the world combined
make grey.

I like the way such tiny stitches
move into two fabrics;
the way they bind through tug and storm;

the way the sewing machine hums as it works,
though no one else but the horses can hear;

the way mothers and grandmothers
reach for needle and thread;
the slow mending
of the ravel.

The Importance of Coffee

God is calling
so I sit in the mountain sun,

warming my skin
in the cool morning air.

I woke to a rush of deadlines,
to-do lists of the day, the week, the century,

but God wanted coffee
with cream,

and illumed through the ravens—
the black caws of aphorisms,

then rocked on the porch
until time began its fishtail weave

in and out, stringing memory
and physical pleasure

through each heartbeat
like current through river rocks.

There is light here.
There is rest to be spooned like tonic.

The world can wait
until God empties His second cup,

and Morning relays
her golden baton,

and River loosens
the spell of her song.

TCU Texas Poets Laureate Series
(TCU Press)

Alamo Coastline

There is no Statue of Liberty in Texas,
no huge lighthouse in the Hill Country
to guide wayward souls out of the dark
and home to safety.

But I met a man today, new to Texas,
and I asked him how he found his way here.
He stopped for a moment as his eyes filled . . .
and said back in '91,

he lost all three of his kids in a house fire.
Said he *had* to leave,
said he needed a place to go
to get away from their ghosts.

And he'd heard about Texas—
how the sky was so big;
how the sun burned pink before it set,
and thought . . . *maybe there,*

he could find
enough space for his ghosts;
enough light
to lead him home through the dark.

For Love and Michelangelo

There is a memory in touch—
lips on a coffee cup,
feet in the sand,
bodies molded together in sleep,
your hand on my leg.

A hand so sure and strong,
it reminds me of standing in the Louvre years ago,
entranced by Michelangelo's slave sculptures.
I just couldn't resist running my hand
up one statue's calf to its thigh—
shuddering at the feel
of such amazing muscle definition in marble.

Guards, with machine guns,
immediately appeared,
not convinced when I explained
how sculpture was *meant* to be touched;
how it comes alive in the human hand.

It's a gesture so old and familiar,
one like the old master himself would have done—
a satisfied smile on his face;

a smile like yours now.
You stroke my skin
as though you've touched every inch of me
in another life;
back when chiseled marble was the photograph;
back when men took the time
to seduce beauty from a stone.

Bursting into Snowflakes

She died at play . . .
— Emily Dickinson

There wasn't a day that went by
when she didn't look into the heavens
and think of him—
her son, her bright, shining son.

He died on that soccer field
so long ago,
in full run;
a slight smile upon his nine-year-old face,

no trace of any pain;
as though his leap for the ball,
was a leap into the fall sky—
never feeling the ground he fell into . . .

his spirit breaking free
like a low, purple-dusted cloud
suddenly . . . *silently* . . .
bursting into the soft, sweet storm
of a million wordless snowflakes.

— *for Anne Baer, to honour the memory of her son, Scott*

Electronic Quills

This is the pen of the modern-day lover,
though email's a tool for the entire world.
But just think of the others, so long ago
who had to catch the bird,
to steal the feathers,
and pool the ink,
and press the papers,
before they could write even *one* word of love.

Oh, how they yearned, with each slow curved letter,
to send their notes flying through the air,
and pin them to the feathers of the gun-shy birds
"I love you," were their words, *"Please hurry back"*
it could take weeks, months, even years.

The world has changed.
It has taken you and I
centuries to come together,
But now I tell you, *"I give you my heart,"*
and it is yours, just 10 seconds later.

But the birds still remember
what was passed down through the ages;
still remember the yearning
written on those pages.
See how they gather, out my window, undismayed—
each one of them singing
the song of your name.

Graveside in Sanger

It was what funeral weather should be—
pale, winter-dead grass;
the mean bite of February
clamping down through your coat,

through your Sunday pants.
Pain inside and out
letting you know
you are still alive.

And the men . . . all those big, Texas men
standing too stiff—
wishing they were anywhere else in the world
in that moment;

all staring down
during the deluge of "Amazing Grace,"
hands hard-fisted behind their backs;
nails digging into their palms;

men who hadn't cried since childhood;
men who had learned from their fathers
how to force their tears down,
through the soles of their restless boots.

Bad Theology

She couldn't convince him
that he was a good man—
a kind man; a *moral* man.

He had grown up spoon-fed
on brimstone and sinnery—
told he was destined for eternal damnation.

So ironic, she thought,
that religion made God's work so much harder;
kept so many good people *away* from the church.

But she hoped God worked His magic out there,
when he was out on the plains—
the morning mist rising off the river;

his long, strong legs
wrapped tight around the warm muscle of the horse—
his breath, rounding in perfect halo about his head.

Indian Blood

Great-Grandma insisted
there was Indian in our blood.
Having crossed from California

to Texas in a covered wagon,
it broke down in Arlington, where
her father built the big house,

which she promptly fell from, head
slamming hard against a milk pail
two stories down. Years later;

completely blind, she swore she'd
heard the scandal whispered—right
there in the house, ears keen beyond

the sighted. Embarrassed, the family
scoffed, offered up four blue-eyed,
tow-headed great-grandchildren

as proof: *Simply impossible*. One
day, she asked me to describe the
sunset, upset that she'd forgotten pink.

I said it was the smell of face cream;
her newborn babies; the roses
climbing the back fence. She

smiled, pulled me close, and asked
if I ever heard flutes in the rush of the river;
if the wind ever called me by name.

Where Moonlight Cannot Tread

For as long as he could remember,
he'd wanted to be just like the moon,
round and white,
some traveler's compass in the dark,
one who inspired great love.
So he worked at it—
thinking moon thoughts,
sculpting himself into moon shape,
soaking in the sunshine each day
to practice glowing in the night.

Millennia after millennia,
he worked and worked
until one day, he became
the exact texture, shape and size
of the orb he had seen every night of his life.
But still he was saddened,
knowing no matter
how hard or how long he tried,
he could never be
as bright or brilliant.

It was then when she found him,
on top of that mountain.
She picked him up, put him in her pocket,
took him home, and cleaned him in her bath,
and set him on her nightstand,
on top of the Bible and Burns
and Birkelbach,
and Neruda's book of love poems.

And that night
as she turned out her light,
and reached over
to feel his roundness once more,
he suddenly felt sorry for the big, cold moon.
For no matter how brilliant it was,
it would never know the dark pockets
next to a woman's round, warm hips,

or her sweet, secret sleep
inside the dark of drawn curtains.

Superman's Birthday

It wasn't that he was hard to please.
In fact, it was just the opposite—
he was so *easy* to be around,
and he appreciated *everything*.
But what do you give the man
who saves humanity on a daily basis?

But even Lex Luthor
didn't know his weakness
for the cream and the meringue.

So she baked him two pies,
and slipped into her favourite brown heels
and lead-free trench coat,
(after all, it was cold and rainy and January)
and took the pies up to his office—
watching him raise his right eyebrow
just slightly
over those dark-rimmed frames,
as he watched *her*
bend over
every man's desk,
and . . . ever so slowly . . .
serve each one of them
a warm slice of coconut cream.

Shattering the Ordinary

(a Superman shadorma)

He tried them,
again and again:
timepieces.
But he kept
crushing them on rogue airplanes
and meteorites.

Once, even,
a thankful city
presented
him a watch.
That one was a gold Rolex—
(it was his favourite).

He forgot
he was wearing it
when the train
had derailed—
it had no chance between steels.
"Damn," was all he said.

But Lois
didn't mind at all.
She rather
liked the man
who donned the ordinary
and then shattered it.

When Texas No Longer Fits
in the Glove Box

Once you unfold a road map of Texas,
your world is changed.

Towns like Falfurrias, Carthage, and Maypearl
suddenly become part of your life,
and once you see them,
you can't go back to
not knowing them.

You *have* to go there—
even if it's just with your eyes
or your finger—
tracing those crow's feet county roads
into unexplored territory.

That's how knowledge works.
That's how knowing works.
Life is expanded; there's *no* going back.
There's no refolding the map.

It's like meeting an alarmingly charming man,
discovering his dangerous detours
and thrilling new paths—
finding unforeseen forks
and magnificent natural beauty.

You'll look up at him and know
that the crinkly arch between his eyes
goes from Childress up to Amarillo,
then back down to Muleshoe;

that the whites of his nails reach
from Huntsville to Jasper;
that his green eyes encompass the metroplex—
from Ft. Worth to Denton to Dallas.

And you can't help but *imagine*
that the crooked hairline
beneath his navel
would run all the way down Highway 281
and across the border,
into dark, exotic Mexico;

or that his lips could take you
on incredible road-trips—
stretching clear across the state—
from El Paso to Nacogdoches
with just a smile.

Or that the best kiss of your life
would whisk you through
the wild-flowered Hill Country,
and leave you
weak-kneed and breathless
along the Riverwalk
in old San Antone.

The Closer

They talked about it often—
about the best way to die, and the worst.

They had seen it all, knew all the signs—
declining urine output, bluing nails,
rising temperature; chain-stoking breath.

But some patients would hang on,
despite these sure signs,
long past the time when their body
should have simply given up;
long past their family's emotional and physical limits.
And that's when they brought her in—
the one they called *The Closer.*

She would fly into the room, clad in bright clothes,
cursing the road, and the traffic; hinting of fresh cigarettes;
and lift that dark, dank room, full of weeping and doom,
with a wicked smile, and an off-coloured joke,

introducing herself irreverently to everyone there—
saying who she was; what time it was;
saying she was there to send everyone of them off—
bon voyage, farewell, arrivaderci, vaya con Dios.

And she would tell the family to say their good-byes,
and go out together, somewhere, to eat or drink or smoke,
or just drive . . .
because *some people just don't want to die
with everyone watching.*

And sure enough they would—every time.
The family would leave, and the dying would die.

So many people asked what the secret was
to her Hospice badge of honour,
but she'd just shrug her shoulders,
and joke in her hard, gruff voice,
"I guess I can just close the deal."

But the day she came for *us,* and told *us* to go,
I lingered, hiding behind the door,
and watched her open the window,

though it was dark and freezing outside.

And she sat by my mother, and gently took her hand,
and whispered something inaudible,
but in a tone so low and heartfelt,
it brought tears to my eyes.

And I felt the sudden swirl of soft breeze;
smelled the perfume I remembered
from so long ago;

and turned my eyes to the opening of the window—
knowing Death had come and swept the room;
knowing her soul had become
the same colour as the wind.

Hanging On

When the Alzheimer's set in
she clung to her coat hangers.

Not the big plastic ones, or the padded girly ones,
but those old, bendable wire ones she had used
every day of her life,
in every load of laundry, in every closet,
on every campout.

She would hug them to her breast
with both arms, terrified to let go.

At night, she would hide the extras
under the mattress
or in the drawers
so no one would steal them.

And in the mornings,
she would put on as many clothes
as she could, layer after layer,
so she could keep the empty hangers in her hands.

The curve of the hook,
the twist in the neck,
the thin triangular labyrinth
held her busy fingers and idle memory
when *our* faces, *our* names could not.

It was the one thing she could remember about her life,
the one thing she could hang on to
that still held purpose,
that could somehow lead her back
to clarity . . .
if she could
just
hold
them
tight enough.

The Monarch and Her Mistress

for Dominique Inge

There was something about her
that stoked the soul;
a rekindling that made the heart beat
a little faster;
the lungs breathe
a little deeper.

Long-limbed and elegant,
old enough to have
walked in beauty,
as well as owned it;
possessing an aura that drew others in
like the irresistible scent of gardenias;
like cool fat grass to the toes.

In God's great plan,
we were made for each other—
the trees, feeding oxygen,
humans, carbon dioxide. . . .
Even the Cherokee call them
the Standing People—
our extended family on this good earth walk.

But it's hard for me to separate The Monarch—
that grand, old live oak in the Inges' garden—
from her Mistress.
Indeed, rarely can I think of one without the other.
Both possess a stillness, a grace
born unto them,
yet nurtured and fed
through the many years
by the constant poetic exhalations
of all those Texas Laureates
who have clustered around
their genteel feet.

Living Close to DFW Airport, September 12, 2001

How often I complained
about airplane traffic;

about the constant noise,
the cluttered horizon,
the disfigured constellations.

And how I cried, that September 12th,
standing in the driveway,
face pressed to the sky—
listening, *searching* . . .

finding nothing but the drop-jaw shock
of Orion.

Woman in the Pipe Shop

Amid the intoxicating scents
of man, and leather,
and sweetened burley,
and latakia,
she kissed him—
a deep lover's inhalation
of lips and breath and tongue—
not realizing every pipe stilled,
every struck match, burned,
every conversation, paused . . .
all dazed in the discovery
of the perfect, unnamed blend
of earth and flesh and fire.

Picking Up the Accent

My husband calls me a chameleon,
says that everywhere I go,
I pick up the accent,
sounding just like a local
within a few months of living there.
I had no idea I did that.

I wonder if it's the food.

But maybe that's what
finding your own voice
is all about.
Maybe it's not so much
about where we're from,
but where we've *been*
that matters.

We ingest every experience.

All those heartbreaks and sunsets
and music and kisses
seep into the bone,
curve the hand around the pen,
streak the hair, deepen the dimples,
and lilt the vocabulary
like quick whiskey to the tongue.
We can't help but bring it *all* to the table.

It took me 2 hours and 42 years to write this poem.

Perhaps one day, I'll travel to the moon
and learn the accent of silence
from the barren craters and powdered Tang,
and mix it all in
with the Florida sunshine and citrus;
the Carolina society and sugar;
the New Orleans *Laissez les bon temps rouler*
and gumbo;
the cowboy boots and Tex-Mex;

(and all those other places I've yet to know)
and *then* see what voice emerges
the next time I come to the table
and sit down to write a poem.

Redefining Beauty
(Dos Gatos Press)

Honeysuckle

It sprang up wild along the chain link fence—thick,
with glorious white
and yellow summer blooms, and green tips that we
pinched and pulled for one

perfect drop of gold honey. But Dad hated
it—hated its lack
of rows and containment, its disorder. Each
year, he dug, bulldozed,

and set fire to those determined vines. But each
year, they just grew back
stronger. Maybe that's why honeysuckle's been
my favorite scent;

maybe that's why I felt the sudden urge to
plant it that one day
in May, when cancer stepped onto my front porch
and rang the doorbell,

loose matches spilling out of its ugly fists.

Spock Thinks I'm Sexy

I'm well aware of what I look like—all
bald and dimpled and brainy in the back,
like something from the Star Trek crew.

I'm well aware, also, that this isn't what you
signed up for. You were always attracted
to my body; to my hair.

So, I'm letting you go. You're completely
free to have a wild affair with some buxom
brunette, someone who's still a whole woman.

Really. Go. It would be easier than seeing that
oh shit look in your eyes when I catch you staring
at me. Anything, you see, is better than that look.

Maybe next September, my scars will have healed,
my hair will have grown back a bit. You can come
and visit, see for yourself if I'm woman enough.

This is tough for a man, I know. But, before you go,
let me extend my right hand, fingers split down the
middle, in traditional Vulcan farewell, and here,

let me extend my left hand as well, middle finger
standing high on its own—for a cultural combination
of good-byes: Live long and prosper, *Asshole*.

Second Spring

for my son, Matthew

My son has grown a look about him—
something green and anxious,
a need to reach beyond the Red River,
beyond the familiar, a need for new eyes

to see him as the man he's become,
instead of the boy he once was—
a long-limbed spider
emerging from a hole,

a cicada throwing its body into song.
Just born, he flailed those arms,
screaming his way into this world,
all legs and lungs.

I see that same look in my own reflection,
opening the windows after 9 months of
confinement—curled on my side, fighting the
cure that was killing the cancer.

I rub the dark from my eyes,
inhale a deep breath of fall—
that second spring of Texas.
I take two keys off the hook by the door,

put them together, on one ring—a final gift
to my six-foot-three-inch baby—still reaching, still anxious—
one key to take him wherever he wants to go,
the other to bring him back home.

Cowboyed Up

My great-grandmother told me stories—how she
walked six miles, each day,
to get milk. Farmed out at eight, she cooked and cleaned
and took care of small

babies for families who could afford the help.
But it wasn't harsh
terrain or hidden rattlers that bothered
her on that journey;

it was the miners she passed, disillusioned
by months of fruitless
picking and panning and homemade moonshine, the
crazed ones eyeing her

like a deep, struck vein. She learned quickly who had
to be fought each day—
kicking, biting when she had to, not daring
to let go of the

precious sloshing buckets. I had always felt
unworthy of her
passionate blood, wishing I'd inherited
a miniscule piece

of her five-foot-nothing grit. My friend, next door,
surprised me today,
said he considered himself strong, until he
saw me go through two

surgeries, and chemo, and radiation;
said he watched me leave
the house every day—big, glittery earrings
hanging stark against

a bare head, a steel glint tinting my eyes, my
feet, bound, *armed* in a
swaggering clomp of cowboy boots—tough, pointed,
ready for a fight.

Redefining Beauty

I could only see a few feet down
then there was a black hole
and I was looking into the belly of a monster.
— Linda Hussa, "Homesteaders, Poor And Dry"

There is this place on the body,
this erogenous zone
that only the bald know—

the lower part of the head,
the place that first touches the pillow,
where the skull just begins its curve up

to cradle the brain; the place where you
put both of your hands, and electrical
currents took me by surprise, and you

pulled me in, your eyes wide open,
and you kissed me, without a hair on my
body, without a hair on my face.

This is the deepest part of the journey,
when we've traveled the dark well down
into the earth's core—

down, where there's nowhere else to go,
down, where Mother Nature's in her kitchen
next door, a pot of volcanoes simmering

on the stove. Down, where no follicle
of sun has *ever* reached, where each
being is blind by divine design, where

two eels wrap thrice around
each other in a dark tangle
of skin on skin, and one leans

into the other and whispers, *You,*
are the most exquisite, most beautiful
creature I have ever seen.

Wee Cowrin' Timorous Beastie
(a 17th-Century Scottish Epic
CD and Book by Lagniappe Publishing
Music composed by Howard Baer)

Wee Cowrin' Timorous Beastie

Come, dear lads, and hear the great story,
an old tale of love, but brimming with glory.
Drumclog of Alba, and a Scottish pirate,
who kneeled before none, save the lass whom desired it.

And she was as fair as a moonbeam caught
in a pond full of lilies that time forgot.
Her beauty was as ancient as dear Drumclog,
and it swirled about her as an illusive fog.

Those all around fought to stand in her wake
for just the scent of her passing caused grown men to quake.
Nobility, she was not—just the innkeeper's daughter,
But with just one glance, any prince would besought her.

And there was something hypnotic about her eyes,
more than the deep colour of midnight blue skies,
They were ample and Learn-ed, and could enter the soul,
seeming to read one's thoughts as an old sacred scroll.

Her bosom was adorned with an extraordinary brooch—
delicate in stature, gems beyond reproach:
An odd striped quartz, an unpolished garnet, and
a citrine that marveled the sun that shone on it.

It trembled and shivered with each kiss from the light,
whether by sun, or by moon, in the depths of the night.
In her essence, it lived, for she wore it without cease.
An appendage it became, of her body, a piece.

Those that knew this fair lass, whose name was Vashti,
came to fear the odd pendant, thought it possessed evil eye.
For years before, a thief had forced from her neck,
this brooch her love recovered, from a witches' ship-wreck.

The thief tore from her throat, not just the jewel,
but the fabric and stitchings of her delicate wool.
And in doing so exposed the rise of her breast,
(which quickened in the cold of the darkening west).

Vashti screamed in soprano, the voice of the young,
but her yell was overtaken and soon outdone
By the terror of the thief, whose hand was a-flame,
But unscorched was the brooch, and tossed back to the dame.

She caught it before it fell to the ground,
It was cool to *her* touch as a river pebble just found.
Many had witnessed this miraculous event,
But some thought the brooch evil, and wished her repent.

But Vashti just smiled as she watched the thief burn,
"'Tis protection from my love," she'd said with great yearn.
She looked to the sea, her heart full of need,
"Soon he'll return. John Murray, Godspeed!"

She turned to walk home, her smile of a faerie,
for she thought of her love and the day they would marry.
Witch thought the masses, but nothing was heard,
they simply crossed themselves there without saying a word.

She noticed no one but a pale little lad
who was staring intently at the brooch that she had.
"Dinna worry, little man. Of yer fears, this least be,
'Tis just like meself, wee cowrin' beastie!"

Hours became days, days became years.
Her longing spawned needs that mixed with fears.
At the sea she was seen oft' at three in the morn
Hair wild and unbound, fist held out in scorn:

"Nay!" she'd shriek, and to tears she'd succumb,
and sink to the sand, her body cold and numb.
She'd spend hours on her knees, for John's return, she'd pray,
just to be answered in sunrise and another new day.

Her pleas to God grew more and more,
yet years still would pass, 'till it was three . . . then four.
In her dreams, she remembered her love at sixteen,
as he returned from his first hunt with treasures unseen:

*　　*　　*

He opened his sack, and laid on the ground,
his first treasure ('twould make the wealthy astound).
"For you, *Queen* Vashti," he flashed his crooked grin,
Aah, he was devilishly handsome, even back then.

"One day, when my wealth would rival a king,
I'll beg for yer hand and place on it a ring.
For I'm denied ye by yer faither, 'till a bounty I've made,
but with these great riches, a ship's fleet can be paid.

"But before ambition, before I leave for the sea,
Keep this one gift, a betrothal from me."
John sifted through the treasure, which clinked like tin bells,
'till his favourite he found, cloaked in seaweed and shells.

In fresh water he washed and rubbed it with his thumb,
'till the muck dissolved and the clarity had come.
And there, in the sunlight, and dwarfed by his hand,
was the most splendid of citrines found in any land.

Held up to the sun, the stone caught every ray,
then turned them to rainbows and into a spray
that sprinkled o'er the lovers and blessed them so priestly.
"But compared to yer grace, lass, 'tis a timorous beastie!"

"Nay, 'tis too much!" Vashti exclaimed,
"'Twould rather have you, John, and the riches of yer name!"
"And one day you will," John whispered in her ear.
He kissed her fair neck; her eyes grew glazed and unclear.

At once, from her depths, came a most delicate moan,
heat seared through his body—flames yet unknown.
Lips pressed to sweet lips, John ascended his hands
into her thick hair, the colour of bright golden sands.

Further in he drew her, 'till they both fell together
into that infinite realm—the love that's forever.
"I wed thee this moment, under God I am yers;
return soon, John Murray, I need nae' riches nor lures."

"As God as my witness, from this very dawn,
I am thy husband!" declared honourable John.
And honourable he was, although quite the rogue,
Vashti feasted in his kisses, and devoured his brogue.

And as he brought her to the brink of her maidenly existence,
he reeled himself in, though it took all his resistance,
for a virgin she was and a virgin she'd be,
when they stood before God and her whole family.

And years he's been gone, he'd be 20 by now.
Would his eyes be the same? Could a man keep such a vow?
Vashti looked in her mirror—but would *he* know *her* face?
Would his imagination take over and give her more grace?

Little did she know, she had nothing to fear,
her beauty simply deepened from year to year.
In John's arms, lived her heart, where it's beating first began:
she's a one-man lass—God help her, Murray's that man.

John Murray began life as a poor lad hisself,
selling Mum's biscuits that cooled on the shelf.
For every pence he'd bring home, his mean Mum would say,
"Ya haven't earned yer sup 'till you've got 10 pence a day!"

It was never enough, though try as he might,
So John left home, his cheek, red from smite.
Wearing only his clothes and the hat on his head,
the sea summoned his name, 'tis where he was led.

For when you're down and hungry, it's best to be courageous,
kick life in the teeth, be loud, be outrageous.
For the meek may inherit the earth one day,
But the defiant embrace it—that's the John Murray way!

What a tale he told on that wet winter morn,
desperate and cold—no jacket to have worn.
But cocky he was with that crooked little grin,

and sold a captain on his pluck—could take it square on the chin.

So the captain employed him, and taught him the ropes,
and the knots, and the sails, and how to read the waves' slopes.
The years passed by, John grew to be the best,
and by sixteen, he knew the ship better than the rest.

So he set out, on his own, in the dark o' the mornin',
but the captain had caught him giving one last warnin':
"Be careful, dear lad, of the ancient ones' curse,
for only the Learn-ed ones touch what's described so in verse.

"Treasures? Aye, but evil call's a spell,
then Donas* hisself crawls out from hell!
Sorcerers *did* bless those Learn-ed riches,
but, if Learn-ed ye not, then leave them to the witches!

Thoir an aire!"**

Murray shook his hand, for he knew where to look;
for the wealth of the ancient he transcribed from a book.
That first hunt was fruitful, and the treasures so great,
that he betrothed dear Vashti, then chased down his fate.

Three vessels he purchased with the gems that he bore,
hiring deck-hands and swabbies with nothing but lore. . . .
Yet they came—toothless and mangled from innumerable sails,
risking body and soul, but the greed prevailed.

So they shipped out with John, Captain at sixteen.
Grown men saluted, though he was still green.
And he worked out a system, where every man's pay
would be tallied on deck at the end of the day.

Captain Murray chose first from each day's plunder,
then rank by rank—each chose spoils from asunder.
The remaining John saved, as a pirate should do
(for wealth of his own bought his love's plunder too!).

---

*Devil

**Beware!*

Aye, that scrawny little lad had learned to read scrolls,
marking ship-wrecks as old as Gaelic souls.
He grew tall and tough, the most handsome of men.
Broad shoulders, baine* hair, that same dashing grin.

John proved a grand Captain, and his men were devoted,
yet he was greater a Pirate, for the galleys were loaded
with years upon years of found sunken treasure,
and when it became more than schooled men could measure,

Captain Murray gave the order, and the ships came about,
on course back to Scotland, (the crew gave a great shout!).
"Vashti, my love," he murmured to hisself,
"Prepare thy heart and thy *bed* for John Murray's wealth."

Aye, the wealth of his bounty, could a small nation buy,
but the wealth of his body was generous to the eye.
His stance was majestic, his bulk loomed so beastly,
nothing about John was wee cowrin' beastie!

The crew danced through the night, devouring much ale,
for they were reaching the end of their four-year sail.
Yet . . . unnoticed by all, was a gathering fog,
only a pirate could sense it . . . like a quiet watch-dog.

It surrounded the ships, hovering so near,
that the world beyond seemed to just . . . disappear.
The morning grey brought an odd feeling of gloom,
for they were trapped on the sea, like a floating tomb.

And on that same day, the rains began in Drumclog
with a ferocity that turned each garden to bog.
Days turned to weeks; the rains would not cease,
Every roof leaked, every crop was deceased.

The food that was stored, turned rotten with mold.
Firewood was useless, the town shivered with cold.
The sheep burst their pens, the pigs soon followed
for the animals could sense the soil being . . . swallowed.

---

*pale or blonde

Seaside was abandoned, the waves ripped down the dock.
It trampled the shelters; scattered livestock.
The bailtean* moved up to the highest farmhouse,
Inhabited by the Retericks and one ailing grouse.

Now we all know the Retericks, for the faither was the one
who shunned John's intentions for becoming his son.
Vashti watched the crowd approach through the drape on
        her pane,
foreboding they looked, murderous, *insane.*

All of them entered, for the farmhouse was great—
the remaining fortress from an old lord's estate.
And dry it was, since of stone it was made,
Even the pigs gathered there, under dry shade.

Once safe and dry, the villagers began to bellow,
"It's not fair that such luck should befall one fellow.
'Tis evil!" they shouted, "For, how can ye explain,
how untouched ye are from this diabhlaidh** rain?"

Vashti heard the commotion and walked down the stair,
each face turned upon her, though she was unaware
that their hearts had become as wretched as the rain,
they intended to make their misery *her* pain.

"'Tis her brooch!" one man shouted, "'tis evil I say!
It has called down God's wrath to our village to stay!"
As he grabbed Vashti's pin, he let out a harsh cry,
For his hand became branded in the shape of an eye.

The same shape of the citrine she protected with her hand.
Vashti realized her peril, for they did not understand.
"'Tis not the brooch that is evil," she explained to the mob,
"but the heart of the man whose intent is to rob,

---

*village
**diabolical, hellish

or to rape, or to murder . . . to do others much harm.
Evil lives in the man, not the beautiful charm."
Vashti lowered her hand, 'till her brooch was uncovered,
its glisten was glorious in the candlelight that hovered.

But the mob was unmoved: "Vashti is a witch!
She has cursed us all with that brooch from which
Donas hisself made in the belly of hell!
God sent it to the sea to keep us all well.

"But Murray brought it back. That pirate must pay!
He brought evil unto us when he pinned her that day.
He will pay with *her* death. His beloved will die.
And we'll bury her along with that damned evil-eye!"

Vashti's faither said nothing, for he was filled with great fear,
that they'd burn all he owned, (and his own life was dear!).
So they took her—he let them—without saying one word,
Her life wasn't worth *his* wealth, he ensured.

So they prod her with sticks, touching only when they must,
the one who flamed flesh with just one single touch.
They tied her to a post in the pen with the swine.
Then declared a great feast with warm ale and wine!

But in drunken haste, they killed too many pigs,
and neglected to prepare them and cook them on rigs.
Dead flesh on the ground, in two days became rotten—
but they ate them in their stupor, for time was forgotten.

Vashti grew weak, but thankful for their ale,
it gave her time to will the wind to bring John back by sail.
Folks grew sick from the pork, rotten to the bone.
Their blood was poisoned; their skin, a grayish tone.

Those strong, made a fire to burn the witch and healthy swine,
(they thought them cursed by proximity)—no longer fit to dine.
The flames grew high, becoming a beacon in the night,
piercing miles of dark fog, to bring Drumclog in sight.

*   *   *

"Land ahoy!" was the shout. All hands ran to deck,
weeks of fog forced the ships to keep speeds in cheque.
And there it was, dear Drumclog, all but calling them by name.
Murray aimed the sloops towards the mighty crimson flame.

"Faster, lads, faster!" Murray kept the sails high,
for his dreams were consumed with his bonnie lass's cry.
The fog was fading quickly, the landscape growing strong,
but his heart felt fear: something was *wrong*.

John walked the shore days later, so long he was away,
but Vashti wasn't there—why was she astray?
Did she take another man? Had she another wed?
His face became ruthless, with murder in his head.

The rain was finally easing when John burst into the pub,
Slamming down a new found coin, he ordered ale and grub.
His heart was raw, his look was mean, the barkeep only shivered,
(he knew he'd die before the morn with the eye *he* was
        delivered).

"What happened here while we were at sea?" Murray asked
        the nervous lad.
"Rrrrains that came from hell's front door, brought on by
        one quite mad!"
Murray raised a single eyebrow, amazed at such belief
that men control the realm of God, like a ship's helm to a thief.

"Aye," the lad continued, happy with the chat,
"at dawn that wwwwitch will burn; she's a beautiful hell-cat!
She wwwwears a brooch of citrine, more grand than any seen,
but to touch it burns the body, but not that devil queen!"

Before the yarn was finished, Murray bolted out the door,
and jumped upon a borrowed horse, and with a vow, he swore
that those who touched his Vashti, would wish themselves
        a death
much quicker than the painful one he cursed beneath his breath.

Into the heart of Drumclog, he raced the panting mare,
she sweat with pace and heavy weight that John forced her
        to bare.
He galloped toward the growing flame—the one that led
        him home,
then slipped onto the muggy ground; soundlessly he'd roam.

Soon he was upon them, the ones who'd damned her dead.
John stalked them mercilessly—removing every head.
His pirate sword was bloody, his eyes were wild with pain,
he had to find his love before the sun would shine again.

The rain had finally ceased, but the fog was heavy still.
John shuffled through the bodies: some lay drunk, others ill.
He called her name in anguish; he would search 'till she was free.
"Where are you, my love, my wee beastie?"

Suddenly, the moon burst through; he spied a tiny spark.
He vaulted toward this shining hope winking in the dark.
And soon he found that glorious gift given at his betrothal,
still pinned to the heart of his faithful lass, both laying in a
        brothel.

"Vashti, my love," John pleaded, "open thine eyes to me.
I shall kill every creature who has put his hands on thee."
His answer was a moan; for consciousness she sought,
"John," she murmured through her breath, "'tis only evil to
        be fought."

He cut her bonds to free her hands; lifted her to his embrace.
She weakly cupped his air-cold cheeks and kissed the
        warrior's face.
In just one arm he held her, and she finally rested there—
for she was in the very place she'd asked for in her prayer.

As he carried her away, cloaked by returning fog,
a hand reached out and grabbed John's arm, like a desperate,
        rabid dog.
"Vashti!" the voice demanded, "Let me see my daughter's face!"

John paused only in respect—'tis a son-in-law's true place.

"Faither?" she whispered, but realized he was drunken thick
    with wine.
"You left me there to burn with just the company of swine?"
"Witch!" he screamed, "'tis all yer fault!" He grabbed his
    daughter's throat,
but John's bloody sword was ready, and both hands did he
    smote.

And as the two appendages dropped onto the soggy earth,
a scream was heard across the town, but was drowned out
    by the mirth
of . . . ceasing rains . . . of rising dawn . . . of a world returned
    to good,
For the lovers were together, as God decreed they should.

Back upon his blessed ship, John nursed Vashti to health,
and brought on board a man of cloth to wed the man of wealth.
And in their vows, John placed upon her hand a splendid ring—
soon coveted around the world from queen to mighty king.

For a king he was, that pirate rogue, for his lass was now his bride.
And that night, John gave her *all* his wealth—t'was nothing
    left to hide.
And her ancient brooch? It twinkled there, in the cool dark
    of the night,
for it had led him back to her; 'twould always stay in sight.

And when they lay together as sacred husband and as wife,
'tis *all* she was wearing: reflected moonbeams of its light.
Drumclog was soon abandoned, most people dying fast,
for greed and lust and hatefulness, all three make cancers last.

And when the land had cleansed itself, and Eden was restored,
John Murray built his castle there—became the rightful lord.
He ruled his people faithfully, always doing what was right.
Enemies knew to give wide berth to those under his sight.

And Vashti bore him many sons to rule in years to come.
And all did own that pirates' rogue (which endeared them
      to their Mum!).
They started out as little lads, but soon came all to bare
that mark of true nobility that those of honour wear.

Still today, in modern times, Scots kin to the north and east be,
none other than the lovely heirs of that wee cowrin' timorous
      beastie.
And that, my friends, *is love*, though seeming small and quite
      afraid,
it rules the hearts of all mankind; and 'tis from what John
      Murray's made.

Becoming Superman
(Zone Press)

Becoming Superman

She thought it was all about the phone booth,
in fact, that's what impressed her most about him—
well, that and the flying thing;
and that one perfect curl.

But it was the *place* that changed him
which fascinated her—
that secret place you go
with your mundane baggage and worries;
that place that strips you down to your skivvies,
and you emerge,
confident,
hands on your hips,
flawless tights,
your cape, restless in the wind,
wearing the colour you *know* brings out your eyes,
stronger,
faster,
ready to leap.

Don't Be Nervous

when you see her.
Don't worry about
what you will say, or
how you will say it.
Just look at her,
and wonder
how your hand will fit
in the small of her back;
how many pins it takes
to hold up her hair.

Teenage, Burning

It was one of those combustible nights—
teenage daughter and final report cards;
seven zeros grounding her from her big
trip with friends—what she's looked forward to all

year. Doors slammed; words, like grenades, she'll only
regret when *she* is 45, when her
own daughter discovers matches. Times like
these, we parents doubt we're qualified for this gig—

it would be so easy to give in,
to give her everything she ever wanted.
Tough love doesn't *begin* to describe it.
Call it *scorching*—passion burning every

exposed heart; my great love for her, groping
for answers while the house is on fire. I
sit on the floor, outside her bedroom door,
listening to her cry herself to sleep.

Texas Longhorns

I always thought them the loneliest of creatures—
perfectly happy to be on their own for days at a time,
and when they *are* together,
they're unable to breech that deadly horn-span
that keeps them apart.
No side by side touching,
no hugs.
Self-sufficient and tough;
smart and gentle.

My father and brother sit at the supper table,
heads down, eating,
four feet of silence between them.
Women come and go and hover and peck
like cow birds,
but *they* need nothing more
than food when they hunger,
the sun on their backs,
miles of barbed wire to mark what's their own.

Ask the Crow

Just ask the Crow.
The Crow and I know
the sanctity of sunset.
We gather here whenever we can—
he on the high branch
me on the low,
hoping for just a *few* clouds
to set the sky aglow with
brilliant oranges
and flaming pinks.

Och! the world spins faster
than the modern man thinks,
for when we still for a moment
and watch how fast the sun sinks
then we know
how fleeting is the day.

Just ask the Crow.
The Crow and I know that these
are the *thin* times between the worlds—
the Angels descend
and the Faeries rise up
and we all gather here
to drink from the cup of magic—
that sweet elixir
few take the time to get to know.

A few like me,
the Angels,
the Faeries,
and the Crow.

Names We've Never Known
(Texas Review Press)

Charmer

There was nothing he couldn't charm.
Standing on the edge of that irrigated
pond, they'd come for him, with three
taps on a Folgers can—water boiling

in anxious catfish. Cattle all but
skipped his way, rubbing up against
him; throwing back their heads for a
scratch, like 800-pound kittens.

Everything and everyone succumbed
to his charms, except Grandma—I
just couldn't figure out their attraction.
Reported to have *never* had a sense

of humour, she seemed impervious
to his devious smile; his rogue ways,
bouncing off her stoic face
like a Ping-Pong ball to paddle;

her flared, lupin eyes, unyielding;
flinting; ready for combustion.
But one summer, after three weeks
of constant rain, I sank, wellie-deep,

in the milkdud clay, and she came,
pulling me out of my boots and
onto her—both of us falling back
in the mud; her laugh, softening

her face like the honeymoon
picture above their bed; her
cheeks, her eyes, bursting
into mounds of bluebonnets.

Atheists

All those people who call themselves atheists
should come on down to
Palo Duro Canyon. Let them walk that thin
trail between rattler

and cactus; let them watch thick canyon walls slide
from brown to amber
to dusty purple; let them stand beneath a
simple, geode night

sky, watching it crack open to a drusy
of stars . . . and *then* let
them ponder the possibility that there
just might be *something*—

some vast, wondrous Being, greater than themselves.

What Goes Unseen

Vocatvs atque non vocatvs Deus a derit
(Bidden or not bidden, God is present)
— Carl Jung

The moon broods over her work,
arms crossed; her back to the night;
oblivious to circling planets;
waxing, waning;

braiding silks of corn; singing
songs of bloom to white, timid
blossoms; pulling up warm, chenille seas to
the chins of cold

shores. The sun pirouettes through
crescent windows; labouring;
dusting curved walls; streaking your hair—your head,
bent down over

open books, unfinished chores.
Always, *always*, there is work
waiting to be done . . . yet . . . Venus circles;
melons ripen;

moonflowers wait for the night.

Snakes

Mom taught me better than this . . .
yet, half an hour spent kissing
your lips, and I'm careless and dazed, easy
prey for fast strikes

from dark corners and back seats.
Later, I'll think of you, as
I reach down into the woodpile, gloveless;
my heart, exposed;

defenseless in open hands.

Summer at Texoma

for the Cathros, Kim, Sandy, Nicki, and Ryan

The clouds call my name; the wind
rolls through my hair.
Cicadas sing to my soul as if my body
wasn't there.

The lake ripples with life. She's cool
as iced gin.
She opens up wide and lets one more life in.

Summer at Texoma.
True-hearted friends.
Words and wine flowing.
Life, lived well,
never ends.

Directionally Impaired

She always wanted
to live in the mountains
or on the coast.
It was *there*
she felt most at home;
there
where she understood
the theory of a compass—
knowing NORTH
would always be
to the right of WEST;
knowing no matter
which direction
she traveled,
sunset would always
lead her back home.

Texas Heirlooms

for my Mom, Wanda Mae Moseley Mann Martin

They called her "Legs" back then—
back in her late forties
back when she worked at Bell Helicopter,
and had to walk clear across Plant 5
to get to her office.

I recall her fluster in dressing—
her detail; her *fuss*
over the perfect skirt hemline—
how it had to fall *just* to the curve of her calves.

And I can see her as I look at my daughter—
something about the shape of the eyes,
the line of the lip,
but further down. . . .

Blue jeans. She *only* wears blue jeans,
fanatic over just the right style, the right cling,
the right length, the perfect back-pocket placement,
inherently knowing how they enhance
those tall, slim limbs.

You told me today, you loved my legs,
as you traced two generations
of long bone and shaped muscle
with your fingertips—
the look of sheer male pleasure
following in your eyes,

and I understood, in an instant,
fashion's impact on society;
understood why Mother
never wasted her money
on fine china
and sterling sugar tongs.

What Really Makes
the Stars Shine

He's learning me well,
plotting my freckles and moles
like Galileo.
The stars glare down, jealous of
my hot skin; his cool fingers

Standing by the Bok Choy
Central Market, Plano Texas

They seemed to grow greener
the longer I stood there, watching them—
the Bok Choy, the celery root,
the green cabbage, the artichokes,
sweetening, ripening, becoming fuller
under the warm touch and rolling accent
of those they had grown up with—
the sounds and the feel
of the fields and the sun and the plow,
wrapped in the brown hands,
and the musical mezcla tongue . . .

The earth and onions know no borders.

They were smiling—
expertly nurtured and picked and cut and stacked.
And I felt unworthy,
unworthy to claim such treasures as my own—
as if a nanny had raised my children;
as if I had no right at the dinner party
to say *thank you*,
when someone commented
on my perfectly *flawless* avocados.

A Rare Man

It took a rare man with an old soul
to see her beauty;
a man whose heart
wandered out in the wilds,
beyond the harsh, artificial glare of city lights—
where the true colour of midnight
could still be seen,
and recognized it
in her eyes;

a man who held the old ways
in the blood of his veins;
who could feel eternity
transcending her Romanesque curves;

a man who communed with the Earth;
a man who, like the crickets,
could still hear the sweet song
that swept between her bare thighs
when she walked.

Austin Embrace

She welcomes with a rush of light;
with busy wide roads, and old tiny green niches;

a home for those needing a place to belong;
a sanctuary for the lost; a mecca for the hungry;

a place where old Texas courts the new;
where art and business shine the same boots;

the place where the cowboy
converges with the rest of the world.

A soap dish of politics and eccentrics and academics,
in an aging limestone lavabo*.

And yet, for all she gives, all she ever asks in return
is that you remember her when you go,

and that you leave the kitchen light on
for the wanderer following behind.

---

*lavabo—a small stone sacred washbowl

Superconductivity

When the two men met,
she felt her worlds collide.

And when they extended their arms
in manly greeting,
she watched,

wondering if their hands
would be thrown apart—
repelled like the opposite ends of a magnet,

or if they would cling together
in a loop of perpetual electrical current
brought on by the rush of recognition—

both having been magnetized
by the steady slow strokes of her skin.

Ultimate Sacrifice

There was nothing she wanted more in this life
than to have a child of her own.

She thought about that
as she lay there, on the table,
beaten—still covered in bruises;
the doctor working the D&C between her legs.

Thirty-three years later,
she still cried that same day, every June,
her body having crossed over
into early menopause;

her womb
having only been given one chance.

An Ordinary Moment
of Extraordinary Beauty
on Northside Drive

The morning after
my family's fourth death
in four months,
I woke from a wonderfully
mundane dream—

a dream about
an ordinary morning;
of finding my children
sleeping in my bed;

of rising, completely rested,
and walking across
sun-warmed wooden floors
and raising the wintered windows
for the first gasp of spring.

And days later,
as the hammering grief
pummeled through the funeral dirge,
my mind drifted back
to something I had seen the day before—

to this *horse*
this untethered, *magnificent*
grey mare

running barebacked and wild
through the streets of Fort Worth,

the musk of the Trinity
flaring her nostrils,
the green of freedom delirious
in her hooves.

Alvarado Coy

my grandfather, Coy Elmo Moseley

He always knew he'd either be a Baptist
preacher or a ditch
digger. It wasn't until he had a few
years under his belt,

and a few Sunday sermons under his hat,
when he realized that
church was full of too damn many women. "All
things equal," he'd say,

"I prefer the company of the ditches."

Crybaby

All day long, I'd keep up with my brother,
to prove I wasn't the crybaby he always
said I was. We'd string trot lines, sing
Paul Simon songs, eat up the ammunition

Grandpa gave us to shoot the moccasins.
Twenty acres of catfish farm, and real guns,
made for the perfect childhood.
But then came the dusk, when we'd haul in

our long-whiskered loot—the cold, slick muscle
of them, curling, whipping, bleeding our hands;
fighting for freedom. We'd carry them in 5 gallon
buckets back to the house—to the sentinel

metal chair and table by the garden hose.
It was my job to hold the light while he cut off
their squawking heads, and de-bone them.
But to this day, I've never learned to clean a fish—

turning my head at each chance of education;
trying to fight back those embarrassing tears—
that surging swell of tender; silently begging for
forgiveness with each wet rip of the knife.

In Your Prime

That's how I'll always remember him—
a crew cut and white t-shirt,
short sleeves snug with muscle;
drawing in the fire of that cigarette,

then tossing it,
like a tiny, opaque bolt of white lightening;
raising that post-hole digger
with two mighty arms,

and slamming it down, deep into the earth,
pulling up a rusted mouthful of ungiving red clay
over and over, until it reached that
perfect fence-pole depth.

All that fire feeding his strength,
arcing his abdomen;
the physical magnificence
of a man in his prime.

He gave up cigarettes years later,
growing old and frail,
succumbing to age;
no longer courting the flame

like you still do—
your hands, guiding it
into the tobacco;
that swell of heat

flaring through your drag.
Your body, your arms—
stallion lean and strong,
reaching for me now

while the fire flows
hot and fierce through your body;
your unyielding lips
tasting like man; like smoke.

The Old That's Worth Hanging On To

There's an incredible old oak tree
just around the corner—
huge trunk, deep roots,
two massive branches
coming out from the middle,

but that last blue norther
ripped one of them off,
leaving the remaining branch
so off-balanced,
so seemingly out of place.

The neighbours all told her
she should cut that thing down,
said it had become an eyesore—
so obviously half of a whole.

But she just shook her head
as she looked across the sofa
to the empty blue rocking-recliner,
picturing the man
who used to occupy that seat,
the man who helped his father
plant that tree.

And further on, into downtown,
there's a white marble memorial
to the Civil War veterans—
complete with
two now-defunct water fountains
one originally meant
for black lips
the other, for white.

And, oh, the civil rights activists
show up from time to time, fists flying,
their media crews in tow,
demanding it be brought down,
calling it an obvious display

of a society ripped in two,
an emotional eyesore.

But the town just sits
and shakes its wise head,
knowing some of the old
should *always* be seen,

knowing some deep roots
are *still* alive and well,
knowing sometimes, *some things*
are too immense to be forgotten.

Horseshoes

There is an elemental
sound in horseshoes—a firmness
when iron hits ground; of strength and foundation.
Double-backed on

your wide, brown mare, it was a
simple ceremony, my
fist full of pale Casablanca lilies
and moonflowers,

then you behind me, the warm
trust of horse beneath us, dressed
in her iron shoes. Generations later,
this is how they'll

remember us, in some old
photo of our reception,
me, barefoot in a puddle of white cloth
and cooling earth,

watching you—concentrating,
poised like Mercury taking
flight—flanges, like tiny wings, at the heels
of your worn boots;

and they'll know those unseen sounds
that follow—that timeless ring
of metal joining metal, then the earth;
those unflinching

arms, ready to catch what falls.

Anniversary

Every night after supper, you stroll these
drought-laden fields, pipe in one hand,

walking stick in the other; making love
to a land as cracked and pieced as thick,

broken glass; only to return smiling—to a
woman, barren for years . . . looking at me

like a crop of sweet corn—green and full
of ripe husks, like sons, too many to name.

Stirring Goldfish
(Finishing Line Press)

The Sufis believe that love is the greatest thing in the
world; that it is the only thing we take with us into the
next world and, in order to know the love of God, we must
first know secular love. So, these poems are a mix of the
sensual and the spiritual; the earthly and the eternal—
love letters interchangeable between God and man.

Circles

Happy are those seeking heaven on earth; who
find those round portals that lead the soul
back and forth. In love, there

are only beginnings, only one circling line.
There is change, there is death, but love has
no end. See how the willows

give themselves to the sun, back-bending to the
earth. See how the moths circle into the fire!
I look into your eyes,

my Beloved, and see the sun and the moon,
and the waltz of lovers . . . all things earthbound;
all things without end.

Wishes

I gathered the seeds of all things beautiful, and
cast them out into the universe, like dandelions.
A deep breath in . . . then blown out.

See how my womb waits for these seeds to
return, with a tiny bed of white down, and a red
lamp, to warm the darkness.

Let us never waste a wish. Let us lie, skin to
skin, beneath the jeweled stars, mouths open,
to swallow their falling magic.

The breath of our love never ceasing, my Beloved;
fists full of thin, headless stems, tossed down—
withering gently at our feet.

River and Snake

See how the river dances with the snake—swerve
to swerve, hip to hip. All that is without end,

arm in arm with a moment in time. Let my worries
break like clay rocks in the tide. Let my heart

know moss violins, and the trilling flute of reed
and willow and fractured bone . . . pausing only,

my Beloved, to shed the stale skin of earth;
to fork-whisper the music of your name.

Redefining Strength

From out of the heavy sea, two great hands
surged with delicate treasure. How could such
fragility exist, unflawed, in the great

turmoil of tide and strife and typhoon? History
and Eternity join hands, casting prophesy and
mollusk into curved pink niches.

Listen to the yearning of the moon; the pulse
beneath tiny gills; the drag of shell across dark
mud; the feeding of one life to the next.

Only you, my Beloved, could give such a gift
of all things living, all things dying, and the
hallowed, sacred song of it all.

Deep Sleep

Sleep is deepest on another's shoulder—
a bridge to the purple mist skies, where
the soul carries a

checkered blanket and a basket full of flowers
to lie in timelessness, feeding its mate with
warm fingertips.

How hungry are those who desire eternal love;
who need the deep of sleep; who believe you
will flare their eyes

with recognition, my Beloved, so they may see the
soul of their lover here on earth—fairie-eyed,
with hibiscus stained lips.

Silence

Earth fills the silence with all things growing.
We sit by the creek; our ears full of creeping
thyme, and blossoms,

and sinking rain. The deep breathing of the oaks,
inhaling our worries, blurring the distinction
between heaven

and earth. See how we burst, like squirrel-deep,
sprouting walnuts! Life is no greater than one
perfect moment.

I hear you, my Beloved, in thick honeysuckle
winds; my heart reaching for you, like the slow
green curl of a fern.

Royal Purple

Every man's heart is equal. There is no
measurement for love—no rank, no biblical
study, no number of crops.

Many men marry, but few know true love—
love that needs no opium; that sits draped in
purple silk, high on the

elephant, and walks through life and death on
thick, five-toed feet; silent and large; faithful
in what it cannot see.

How blessed are we, my Beloved, to have
found such rare love, let us keep it spoiled in
royal purple and sweet apples.

Lifting Up

The greatest of men own the greatest of faith.
See how he lifts his chin to the rancid sneer of
fear! See how he

takes a step closer! See how he inhales its
curling breath; how he raises his hands to
defend! And great is the man

who knows the gift of mortality. He chisels his
name in the sunlight; caresses his love while
the moon arcs by.

He lifts all things up. Your rugged fists of
battle open to me, my Beloved, and swarms
of butterflies sing about my face.

Faith

Fear can suffocate a man. It slithers in, black-
fanged, wrapping snakes of darkness around
our chest! Oh, there's no room to breathe!

But the tiger of faith is fear's greatest enemy.
See how he creeps in on silent padded toes;
see how the stare of golden eyes

loosens fear's hold! The breath of sweet life!
Faith is a great cat, with rasping tongue, who
sleeps, ears twitching and soft against

our thighs. I wait for you in the night, my
Beloved; the open door, creaking in the wind;
a bowl of pale cream, warming on the step.

Rush

Modern men rush like wild rivers—in chaos and
speed—consuming days and nights like loose
pebbles on the ground. How do we

slow such turbulence? Our life is tied, kite-tailed
to the hands of time, whipped from shore to
riverbed to rocky cleft. We hang on to

each other through flood and tide and August
drought; your hand, secure, never slipping; never
leaving mine. Let us ride these rivers to the

infinite ocean, my Beloved, to rest in calm waters.
You dive deep, surfacing again and again;
your mouth full of pearls.

Ready

Only a fool has no fear of the caged lion. He
sees him there, behind the bars, and casts
insults through the iron.

He shaves his mighty mane and taunts his
nakedness! But he mistakes the lion's patience
for submission.

See how the lion's golden eyes hold steady,
unflinching. All the powers of the wild seethe
ready and tense beneath his skin.

Let us study our foes, my Beloved; let us stretch
our clawed limbs and stay strong in our
afflictions—hungry for freedom's open latch.

Hope

I met you when the trees hung heavy in white
blooms, captivated by your voice in the silence.
I opened the window, and left long hairs
for your

nest, and dressed a cage in orange silks, with
a mirror for you to preen, and a bowl of soft,
fat raisins. But greatness, like yours, was
made for

the wind. I hear you now, before the world has
stirred; from that same open window; my tears
fed by your warble on this dark side of
the earth.

It's you, my Beloved, your magnificent song,
singing into my heart: The sun is coming.
The sun is coming. Do not fear; the sun
is coming.

Joy

Hands cannot hold these great sums of joy.
They mount in weightless bricks of sunshine
around us; they stir,

like camouflaged redbirds in the thicket; they
thrum like honeybees, through tiny white pear
blossoms. In thanksgiving,

we feed each other, filling our cheeks with the
delicate pulp of mandarin oranges, our lips
and eyes, brimming-over.

Your joy embraces me, my Beloved, our hands,
perfumed in citrus, wrap tight around each other;
holding nothing . . . holding everything.

Peace

Summer comes through thin, solstice sheers,
her pale blue musk of distant rain, whetting
desires of man and calf. She makes no
apology for her heat—

turning hay to gold as she passes; reclining
deep and hot on exposed shelves of limestone.
But see how cattle sink, uncomplaining, into
spindly mesquite shade,

knowing Sun means them no harm. Trials and
fear and drought may consume us tomorrow,
so let us take this moment, as shadows pass
across our faces, and lie

too close together, my Beloved, in the half-curl
of bovines; balancing this fire that gives and
takes life; thinking only how sweet ran the
creek, our last deep muzzled drink.

Wanting

Each creation in this world is made of love, and
love wants us to have everything we could ever
hope for. A dandelion alone, holds

a hundred wishes. Birthday candles lay waiting
in kitchen drawers. Eyelashes fall as
delicate as shooting stars. We lay

beside the river, giant cottonwoods hovering
over us, as though we were twins in a crib; their
gentle, white seeds, snowing down upon us.

Let us open our hands and catch them, my
Beloved, as Earth cries sweet mother tears; let
us never stop reaching; let us never waste a wish.

Returning

There is a return in the universe; a movement
that never ends; an unforgetting; a stepping out
of the ocean—only to be

welcomed back into the next wave. There is no
end to love, and once known, impossible to be
without. All things return

to love and be loved—like the icicles, marking the
long winter nights; like the purple summer phlox.
I shall take your hand,

my Beloved, be it this world or the next; a hand
that knows the warmth of my cheek; a hand that
knows my circling soul.

Hometown, Texas: Young Poets & Artists
Celebrate Their Roots
(TCU Press)

Leaving Brenham

What is the word for love of the road?
I am neither hitchhiker, nor trucker, nor gypsy,
yet the road has a song of Her own,
an irresistible Siren in every shade of grass,
every barn silhouette, every arch of oak.

She called me here, where Texas declared Independence,
filling my truck with roses, my camera with cattle.
Here, where side roads lurk like lust,
my map curls, soft and wrinkled as an old love;

And my Muse calls again, from just over the next ridge,
in a voice clear as moonlight:
Come . . . come . . . there's something you should see,
someone you should meet,
some story to be told . . .
each EXIT, Her sultry command.

Traveling with Dog

We took her down to Laredo
and stopped just south of Devine,
where cactus clumped like mistletoe
on the railroad and fencepost line.

And we joined the calm of the Night;
the silent stirs of the wild;
till the Moon dawned the horizon
with only a sleepy half-smile.

Then she laid back her wolf-boned head,
and howled to the wind and sky,
untranslatable, yet so sweet—
a love song we couldn't deny.

Tarantulas locked woolly arms;
our lips brushed, tussled, then sparked;
and rabbits down beneath our feet,
made love in the deep burrowed dark.

Making Peace with Scorpions

I learned they *always* traveled in pairs;
they mated for life.

And when one walked across my path,
dozens of babies high on her back,

one fell off, and she stopped
and turned—her long, venomous tail

gently scooping it up, tucking it back
on its perch . . . my heart clicked open.

That night, I dreamed of a scorpion
with an *ohm*-shaped tail; and the next day,

as we walked together, shadow to shadow,
on top of those Marfa mountains,

marveling at the endless view, and the millions
of chalcedony and agate at our feet,

I wondered how I *ever* could have cursed
a creature with that much God in its eyes.

Bowie Snow Globes

> *Have you ever wished for an endless night, lassoed the moon*
> *and stars and pulled that rope tight . . .*
> —Pink

Maybe it was the best cup of coffee
I've had on the road,
or because the entire town took flu shots
at the Dairy Queen.

Or maybe it was all the smiling men;
or that Jupiter
was closer to Earth than it's *ever* been;
or that my birthday

was the day before—the first cool evening
of the season—stars
sparking crisp and tight; or that the air was
intoxicating—

a mix of cedar and cattle and night.
I rolled the windows
down; the moon-roof, open, and circled rounds
in those downtown lanes—

slow figure 8s, not wanting to let go;
the old *RODEO*
limestone gates waiving me homeward; each street-
lamp, a globe—aglow

in white light, spinning crickets like black snow.

Danny Keough

In 7th grade, it was all about
the fitting in, not the sticking out,
but the most important thing, no doubt,
was a class with Danny Keough.

And my, *oh my*, what a handsome lad
who could look your way and make you glad
that a boyfriend you would never have
to compete with Danny Keough.

Now all through school, I was the girl who
made the grades but lacked the looks to twirl
a boy around her smile—not his type—
in the world of Danny Keough.

But life has its great ups and downs—
we moved away, another town,
but came back to spin just one more round—
a chance to dance with Danny Keough.

The time was right, with nothing to lose,
I asked him, "Please, would you please choose one
dance with me?" Oh . . . would he refuse? . . .
but then he *touched* me . . . *Danny Keough!*

Now, all the girls were just bug-eyed but
fate was truly on my side, for the
next slow song was an eight-minute ride
in the arms of Danny Keough.

"Stairway to Heaven," the song that thawed
my heart to men, leaving me in *awe*,
that someone like him would dance with me—
Oh my God!!! with Danny Keough!

So let this be a lesson to all,
they may say no, or you may fall, but
before it's our last curtain call, let's
risk the world for Danny Keough.

Calling the Cattle

We humans have a love of cattle—
with bodies thick and bells that rattle;
with skinny tails made just for whipping;
and busy mouths all wet and dripping;
and furry ears that keep on thinking
they're hearing windmills spin for drinking.

But one time when they needed drinking,
their ears were pricked—such thirsty cattle.
They heard a sound that got them thinking—
a long snort snort; a little rattle—
could this be some cool water dripping?
They looked around through winds a-whipping,

and followed close those sounds a-whipping—
could these sounds lead to cattle drinking?
And then they ran, their wide mouths dripping,
Angus, Longhorns, all breeds of cattle
who came because of all this rattle,
water was calling, they were thinking.

But it *wasn't* what they were thinking.
And yes, they heard some winds a-whipping,
but what, they found, in this great rattle,
was not just water for their drinking,
and in surprise to all the cattle,
was just a human, wet and dripping!

And in a tub! Her long toes dripping!
But she was sleeping, and not thinking
about her sounds, which called the cattle,
who raced to find *no* windmill whipping,
and more than water just for drinking,
but *snoring*, what a vicious rattle!

And oh, how loud! Those doors did rattle!
Her long toes kept the water dripping.
But those great bovines wanted *drinking*,
and put their boney heads to thinking

how they could move that girl by whipping
their tails—oh, mischievous cattle!

Rattle woke her . . . *RUN!* she was thinking
and jumped out, dripping; wet hair whipping,
and left her tub for cattle, drinking.

Passion, Art, Community: Denton, Texas, in Word and Image
(The City of Denton, Texas)

Fun

Picture of Denton woman in the Courthouse Museum B-051

Vacation?
What is that word?

Why would we leave,
when there are crops to tend,
cows to milk,
venison to dry and salt?

See my life in this tintype,
my face aged by the sun,
my eyes full of breached calves,
Indian raids, typhoid caskets.

And where would we go—
we barely made it *here*,
across the Red River . . .

No. I will have no fine china,
no silver for my granddaughters,
but I will give them this land—
this beautiful land tamed by my back,
worked by my hands.

Fun?
Fun comes Sunday mornings at church,
or at night around the fire, telling old
stories; working on riddles of survival—
like how many trees it takes
to keep us alive;

how many logs must be split
to get us through till spring.

The Last Raid, 1874

They were a people in turmoil—
forced out of their hunting grounds;
their very existence threatened by

this white man and his Yellow-Boy weapons.
So they fought back,
stealing their horses,

attacking their settlements,
scalping their women and children.
Mr. Huff wasn't home that 24th day in August

when the band of Keechi
crept up to the ranch, silent moccasins
printing the earth.

Mrs. Huff and one daughter were found first,
their blonde hair scalped. The other daughter
lay out in the yard, dead, yet unscalped. . . .

Perhaps her hair fell over that red man's hands—
hair black as the evening crow's; hair as beautiful
as his daughter's.

And up in the sky, a kettle of vultures
began to stir over the carnage.
Suli, they were called—

Peace Eagles.
From their view, he must have thought,
she would have looked like his own.

Capital Punishment

*History and Reminiscences of Denton County by Ed. F. Bates.
Page 107 notes that a mysterious man was found hanging on the
west side of the Square with this very note pinned to his back*

*This poem was written for the Denton book. It was not
included in the final manuscript but is an author favourite!*

Early one morning
on the west end of the Square,
swinging from a tree, to atone,

a dead man hung—this
pinned note waving in the air:
"Caught riding a horse not his own."

Hickory Creek

Stopping to take a picture of the high water rushing of Denton Creek, October, 2009. Many wrecks happen down there, so I've always told my kids, "Don't Go Down to Hickory Creek."

History & Reminiscences of Denton County *by Ed. F. Bates. Pages 125–132 talk about Sam Bass hiding out down there, rumoured to have buried all his gold from the train heist. His famous mare's name was Jenny.*

Don't go down to Hickory Creek
The current is swift, the danger runs deep
Moccasins hide where the brush hangs back
Dark, gliding angels, silent and black
Don't go down to Hickory Creek

The current is swift, the danger runs deep
Down where Sam Bass hid out for a week
Don't go hunting for the *shanghaied* gold
From the east-bound Union Pacific Railroad
The current is swift, the danger runs deep

Down where Sam Bass hid out for a week
20-dollar gold coins lay somewhere discreet
Buried in the mud to cover their glare
By a tree, marked, for his dear Denton Mare
Down where Sam Bass hid out for a week

20-dollar gold coins lay somewhere discreet
A mystery that's never quite been complete
Don't go down where the Hickory bends
Don't take your fair lover; don't double-dare your friends
20-dollar gold coins lay somewhere discreet

It's a mystery that's never quite been complete
Don't go down to Hickory Creek
Many say it's just a myth—too often retold
Say Bass gambled it all, knew he'd never grow old
It's a mystery that's never quite been complete

Don't go down to Hickory Creek
Down where Sam Bass hid out for a week
20-dollar gold coins lay somewhere discreet
A mystery that's never quite been complete
Don't go down to Hickory Creek
The current is swift, the danger runs deep

New Icaria

History and Reminiscences of Denton County *by Ed F. Bates*
pages 81–84

Reflections of Icaria *by Mabel Schweers, Vol. 7, No. 1, Spring*
2004, pages 6–10

Texas State Historical Association Online Handbook of Texas
Written for, but not published, in the Denton book.

In theory, the idea sounded perfect—
every person living and working
up to their highest potential, each one

giving to one pot; one socialist society.
"All people need," wrote Etienne Cabet, "is a perfect
environment to reach a perfect community."

He had been in France, heard old man Peters talking
about his colony in Texas, a land ripe with beasts
and fertile soil and hungry people.

So, he purchased a 10,000 acre tract from Peter's Land Company,
a land grant of their own on the edge of Denton County,
then sectioned it off to settlers.

But after one year, he succumbed to defeat.
New Icaria was abandoned.
The railroad came through later, settlers even naming

the town after the chief engineer, Justin Sherman.
But in his defense, Cabet's philosophy was only
a *little* off—for how could he realize

perfection, to a Texan,
isn't the absence of our flaws,
but our *embrace* of them.

And nothing in Cabet's world
could have *ever* prepared him
for a land so hard-fisted and wild;

or for a people as tough as Texas bulls—
no philosophy could ever tame;
and no Frenchman could *ever* ride.

An Old Photo of Young Men

Picture of Denton boys in the Courthouse Museum 90.46.22
Written for, but not published in, the Denton book.

We could say they were up to
no good—the flash capturing
a moment of time—that quick light upon
their pale faces;

a glimpse of mischievous
testosterone. Yet we see
them much like ourselves—our great-grandfathers
the same age as

our sons. See how they differ—
the vogue of hat, the button
of vest. See how they mirror—devious
half-smiles of lip;

anticipation, like fire in their eyes.

May Comes to Denton County

Written for, but not included in, the Denton book.

in a sprinkling of ponies;
horse ranches littered with tiny
sunning foals, their mares grazing
close by. Children, sensing the

end of school, bolt, like thirsty
herds to water, running crazed
into three hot months of flip-flops
and late bedtimes.

And on Saturday nights, girls
don eyeliner and short dresses;
long legs wobbling in mother's
heels, like eager, newborn colts.

Small Town Bees:
a poet's thank you to Denton, Texas

I've always heard about the horrors
of small town living—
how everyone knows
everyone else's business

Wasn't it just yesterday, when we, ourselves,
said how the new neighbours
must be doing a lot of remodeling
as all the trucks were coming and going?

It's the drone of bees
in the blooming Bradford pear trees—

you walk outside,
and stand still for a moment
trying to identify that sound . . .
that vital, living, buzz of community
and interaction and gossip
and worship and business and creation—
the stir of making honey—

Wild bees in spring

But when you *need*
when you've had
your third family funeral in three months,
who else would show up with
a cooler full of beer and Dr. Pepper
and flowers and hot brisket and spinach lasagna
and pimento cheese sandwiches?

Who else but these busy bees
would acknowledge your breach of etiquette—
that no *thank you* notes were ever sent out
from even the *first* funeral—
but who instantly forgive,
because they, of course, *know* the reason why:

your overwhelming grief trifecta

and you would eat the brisket
and drink the iced Shiner
and let this comfort fill you from the inside out
and be thankful

and you would let it slip out to the Queen herself
how you wouldn't have made it without them;

how you couldn't *ever* imagine
living anywhere else in your life

8 Voices: Contemporary Poetry of the American Southwest
(Baskerville Publishers)

Palindrome

Today, I am learning to be Dog—
waking when my bladder rumbles,
or when I thirst, or hear footsteps,
or when the blue sky is too irresistible to wait.

I have to go out now.

I want to nose and bless
each tire and tree;
feel unfiltered frenzy over squirrels;
give in to *every* temptation.

And I shall sit when I pause,
executing the perfect *Down Dog*,
and stare
and sniff the wind;

not worrying once
about the dog shit back home
on the carpet.

Because what matters most
are those French fries on your plate,
and the sun on my fur—

feeling a peace
that stretches every hour into seven;

a holiness that makes me think,
each time you say the word *God*,
that you are, somehow,
calling my name.

The E Ticket

The Hospice House

The room starts to get stuffy,
the oxygen machine—
white noise against the shuffle;
whispers and giggles
of gathering angels—
wings tucked like hearts at their backs.

Others arrive
as an odd anxiousness balloons;
six beds in queue,
waiting like portals
to whisk them into the next life;

rectangular roller coasters
into the unknown.

One room over,
someone's ride has begun.
Hear them all—
hands up and screaming.

Tree Blossoms

March winds snow petals
with each gust;
white jewels in my hair, my tea.

Twelve years of drought
have brought her here—
tiptoe roots stretching deep

into hidden waters;
kinking garden hoses
to trickle in the night;

pouring every extra cup of ice
and bathwater at her feet
to make it through till spring,

when tornados, like swirling demons,
try to crack her trunk;
sever her limbs.

Torturous storms beget each blossom;
there is hunger and burden and need;
don't think beauty easy.

Persephone, the Bear

A 911 call about a bear in a kitchen,
and the firemen dispatched,
setting a trap with peanut butter . . .
and there she was.

It was the closest I'd ever been
to a bear—her gentle brown eyes
and triangle head;
her massive claws.

A summer of drought and fires
brought her down,
this goddess of Spring,
lured by hummingbird feeders

and dog food,
and a bowl of pomegranates
on the other side
of that cabin door.

It was protocol—
a trespassing bear was caught,
tranquilized and tagged,
then taken out to the wilderness

and inflicted with fear—
what the firemen dreaded—
yelling, throwing sand bags,
branches, stones,

firing shotguns; revving chainsaws;
then releasing trained bear dogs
to chase her back,
up into the mountain,

hopefully to never return;
knowing if they failed,
and *Brown Bear 377*
with the yellow ear tag

was caught again,
she would be killed . . .
the blood still fresh in the cage
from the last captive.

Ah, let the angels comfort her,
help her to forget the crunchy,
the salt and the sweet
of the underworld;

let her live to tell great grand-bears
about the cruel devils down there;
their lusty, forbidden foods;
those horrible, hellish hounds.

Motel

For where your treasure is, there will your heart be also.
—Luke 12:34

Some may think I've lost my way,
calling this a place of ill repute—
human beings coming together,
a touch of lightning;
a transformation of two
becoming one.

Sometimes the soul needs
a little tango.

Thin sheets pulled up, hair tussled;
sharing chicken salad on beer bread
and a plum from a paper sack;
the juice on your chin,
a siren's song; a plunge into your depths . . .
and I'm lost again;

the forsaken fruit, half-eaten on the nightstand;
its jeweled heart, exposed.

Sign Language

His was a generation
that nearly outlasted the
next—burying
all but two of his seven girls before
he turned 90.

Years ago, with no hopes of
an heir for his fields, he sold
that Chico farm,
took up wildcatting; the untimely swing
of chain against

spinning steel, dropping fingers,
one by one, into oil black
holes—a part of
him buried first, like it should be—one for
every daughter.

One Night in Florida

I want to tell you something I've tried to say for 23 years;
about one night on the Ft. Pierce Inlet,
in a 17-foot sailboat;

how youth and bluster and braying music
finally yielded to a silence
as rich and deep as the blackberry sky,
with only the slap of current against the curved bow;

how I spied a dolphin alongside the boat.

I want to tell you how he looked silver in the moonlight;
how I reached over the side, near the surface of the water;
how he rose to my palm, letting me stroke his long, slick
back
again and again, each time he surfaced.

I want to tell you that after he swam away,
I held my hand up, in the dark,
and looked at it,
as if it had changed;

and how, from that day forward,
I have never lived an ordinary life.

Constant State of Leaping
(The Texas Review Press)

Weeding

> *I generally avoid temptation unless I can't resist it.*
> — *Mae West*

Hunting for agates,
I found the perfect crystal
in a nest of prickly pear,

but hesitated as I reached out,
sensing him lurking,
patrolling his dangling fruit.

Weeding the flowerbed,
I sensed him *again*,
coiled in some hidden niche,

though I beat the ground,
and shook the bushes,
finally spying his curled skin,

tossed like a minute, exotic scarf.
What *kind*?
What kind doesn't matter—

I am *woman*.
He is *snake*.
Our history is tempestuous; complicated.

But I can *feel* him
like the still air before the sky breaks open;
or the pull of the witching stick

from the palms of my hands—
whispering *water, water*.
But he is here . . .

close enough to flare the tiny hairs
on my neck; the amaryllis
apple-red between us.

A Perfect Night at the Observatory,

learning about Big Dipper, Crow,
Orion; a flawless, cloudless
sky—a moon that just wouldn't rise . . .

and I turned to watch *you* watching
the stars—you, my Earth, my rock; *you*,
my North; my steadfast star of night.

What Real Men Do

He was in the Corps at A&M,
in the *Cavalry*,
back in 1929;
back when it was
a man's world,
and a man had to
constantly prove himself
strong and fearless.

And on Friday nights
when the moon was bright,
they would sneak out of the dorm
with their baseball bats,
and head down to the neck
of the muddy Brazos,
and club the wild gators
just for fun.

Adytum*

Michelangelo said he could stare
at a raw block of marble
and see the figure pushing to emerge.

And there is a woodsman I know
who swears he can pick up a tree branch,
and feel the throb of hawk or bowl or saint
begging for his knife;

Each man must labour for the sacred.

I yearn for the creek,
to sit a while,
to learn the stillness of the trees;
the green of vines;

and soon, rocks lift their eyes;
fish rise and tumble from the water;
choruses of birds
crescendo and fall like tiny leaves;

and I begin to feel a thick holiness
looking into *my* soul.

I wonder what God sees
beneath this clamour;
this brush;
this rock hard heart.

---

*adytum—an inner shrine; a sacred place the public is forbidden to enter

You Don't Know Hot

until you've seen August
in Texas,

her full skirt, flaring
as she settles in,
knotting her hair each night
in a low, golden ball;

laying back, stretching long
legs of sky

eastward; pink toenails
of clouds. Cowboys stop
and stare, Stetsons pushed back,
falling in love *again*;

slow exhales of *whistle*
from their lips.

Winter

Every season boasts its beauty,
but I love it *now*,
leaves raked and bagged and blown;
trees, stripped of blonde,
without pretense,
elegant in their stark brunette stance—
nests, like secret hairpins.

It's the time of revelations;
contemplations of simplicity—
a room, a lamp, a chair;
stew on the stove;
nests built one twig at a time
to cradle hearts, tiny and warm.

Letter to the Grim Reaper

for Mike Semler

Seriously?
Is *this* what we should expect?

Sneaking into the night
without knocking;
barging in the bedroom
while we sleep?

Dishes are piled in the sink.
The yard is two weeks past mowing.
The electric bill has yet to be paid.

For God's sake, he was only 50 . . .

Can you at least give us
a little warning—
a wee headache before the aneurism;
a few arm pains before the heart attack

that we may straighten up a bit,
toss the vibrators,
clean out the medicine cabinet,
burn the old love letters.

Ladies and Gentlemen,
this is your life—or rather the end of it.

Mr. Reaper does not care about
what's in the oven,
or the wet clothes in the washer;

his pocket watch says *now.*
Now.

Let us, collectively, turn off the porn,
and water the plants,
and fill up the cat's bowl
before we lay down to sleep.

The Making of a Hero

It is surmounting difficulties that makes heroes.
        —Louis Pasteur, French chemist and microbiologist

When you get a little older, you'll see how easy it is to become
lured by the female species.
                —Batman (to Robin)

I met him on the steps of Willie Pigg Auditorium—
this boy, this beautiful boy, three years older, Adonis
dark and tall, amazed that he was looking at *me*.

The next day, a note passed through his younger
brother, and we were fast in the current of first love,
clinging to each other till I packed up for college;

leaving him to his career—a fledgling fireman.
Home for Spring Break, standing in the frame
of his new house, he spoke of his bank note,

and 50 years tumbled in my brain like barrels
down a waterfall. I watched him talk, excitement
darting his long legs room to phantom room,

this boy, this beautiful boy, so ready for honeymoons
and mortgages; the beams between us, an instant
log jam; knowledge ascending upon me like a sudden

serpent . . . and everything changed. I became his
femme fatale—the one who'd cause him to dare fate;
to charge deep into the flames; his bittersweet catalyst

from human to hero. Standing on the concrete foundation,
I took him to my breast, crying in our moment of sweetness,
knowing one day too soon, I would break his beautiful
heart.

        —*with love for Stephen Malley*

Passing the Gauntlet

He never learned the language of love,
having grown up in silence at the supper table;

their only interaction, the names and scores
and stats of players and teams.

It's what he knew; what his father knew.
But on Sunday afternoons, they'd take to the yard,

two well-rubbed leathers, soft and tended and creased;
that baseball, bridging glove to glove; binding

father to son. Their arms, the air, the *catch* . . .
saying everything they needed to say.

Walking Out

A man of technical precision,
he taught himself electronics—
each fascinating detail

of gears and volt meters;
the secret workings of everything
from toasters to helicopters.

But one day, a trench dug,
pieces of sprinkler system strewn
about the yard, he felt his gift

pack up the sterling of his mind
and walk out,
like an ungrateful vagrant.

I went to see him today,
every one of his clocks, haphazardly
chiming at odd times; five years of

remote controls, face down on the table,
backs off . . . two simple batteries,
helpless in his hands.

Midnight on the Roof at Villa Velleron

There would have been no lights in the 14th century,
but these walls were here—some fellow crazed poet

out on this very same ledge, succulents hedged between
terracotta tiles; lumber at least 500 years old when

it was cut and scrolled for beams and olive presses.
He would have lived with a found cat named Chaz;

drank wine from vines planted by ancient Greeks—
both of us, glass in hand, seeking solace from these empty,

smooth-trod streets; the dark, Luberon Mountains,
a sleeping god; the same virgin moon in our eyes . . .

counting these bells that *always* cry twice—once for the lovers
of the shadows; once again, for the lovers of the pen.

Breathless

To all you men
who love women with curves—
thank you.

Thank you for calling us sexy
when you *aren't* having sex.
Thank you for the winks and whistles
and trucker horns.

Those poor supermodel hips
couldn't bear a boy,
three times his year's weight
(starting high school football
in the eighth grade).

She couldn't handle
your smoked ribs,
or date night at the hockey game—
foot-longs with jalapenos,
and a Coors Light
every third pass of the beer vendor.

Maybe we were built to be
your comfort in winter's dark;
breasts that buoy in the lake;
that warm you in bed.

Thank you for liking
our amplified cleavage—
with and without a bra.

Thank you for pulling us close;
for making love sober,
in the daylight;

for coming up behind us
as we scowl in the mirror,
and kiss our neck, and tell us
our beauty
leaves you breathless.

Good Saturday

The risk of having children
— *Walt McDonald*

In a hospital bed, tubes spiking out of his head,
he reached for me, crying;
though I couldn't pick him up as they tended

to him . . . my love; my child who almost died.
Nobody ever talks about Good Saturday, though
there was nothing *good* about it for Jesus, or Mary—

she probably didn't even get out of bed,
succumbing to exhaustion from the night before,
to see her child, her tender, gentle child,

mocked and beaten and nailed and crucified;
holding His lifeless body in her lap.
And, oh, in those hours, those long, horrible

hours, did He look down, the boy in Him searching
for her face; whispering in his pain
. . . *Mom*. . . .

Oh, the great *risk of having children!*
A child, in desperate need
yet we're powerless to help;

unable to do anything
but touch his bare foot,
and call out the magic of his name.

Contemplating the Nut

Totally disgusted at the funeral home's
used car salesman techniques,
my father decided to shop around for bargains,
finding an irresistible "deal" at Caskets 'R' Us.

A deal so good, he wanted two—
one for Grandma's immediate use,
and one for him,
to wait for years
in his garage, lid open,
disguised as a planter box.

Centuries ago, Italian nuns carried
all their earthly possessions in a trunk
at the end of their bed,
and when they died, it became their coffin.

I rather like that idea—
using such beloved lumber—
touched and worn smooth over the years;

lying down inside when it's your time to go,
a pillow under your head, maybe one between
your knees, skin against real wood—
plain pine or oak;

then buried beneath a walnut tree;
knowing those roots would stretch down
to sup whatever nourishment they needed;
pulling you up into their limbs

to feel the tiptoe of the beetle,
the clawed fist of the crow;
pushed into tiny balls at the end of the branches
to well up as walnuts;

falling at the feet of one who picks you up,
holds your wooden world in his hands,
contemplating softened edges;
the sweet stillness curled inside.

Whisper in the Winter

Whisper in the winter
when clouds hang low and gray,
for Mother Earth sleeps sweetly
in her icy negligee.

Disturb her not with shovels -
don't insist that she awake—
for even rain has hushed its touch
with every tranquilized snowflake.

When the last leaves fell
Earth breathed a sigh,
curled up, and closed her eyes,
and slid to peaceful slumber
while the wind sang lullabies.

Whisper in the winter
her night is cold and deep.

Whisper in the winter
women need their beauty sleep.

Letter to an Old Love

I saw you at your mother's funeral.
I'm so sorry—
I adored her.

I wanted to tell you
you look good;
you've grown into a handsome man
from that boy I knew so long ago.

I couldn't help but stare.
Your children have your eyes.

I learned the North Star
isn't due North anymore—
too many earthquakes
have thrown the world off its axis;

like 30 years ago,
when one word shifted the universe.
I swear the earth trembled
as I walked away;
the night sky
never quite the same.

The Eternal Life of Poets

I do not know, dear reader, what year this will reach you,
but it's 2012 here, heavy with July's heat,

and I am lying on a sailboat
beneath a Night so moonless and clear,
the stars glisten on Her black velvet corset.

Time has no meaning to the stars.
It's taken some of them hundreds of years to reach our eyes—
beginning their journey when Sappho and Dante and Shelley
were alive . . . pen in hand . . . like me.

Know, dear reader, that I lived, and I loved—
Oh God, how I loved!
Earth steadied my feet above her head;
the wind carried my breath;
rivers offered my pale belly,
like a babe, to the sun.

We are thick, now, with people;
light pollution smokes the heavens;
but every once in a while, like tonight,
the old magic shines through.

I wish this for you, my friends—
a soul-filling simplicity;
slow days upon the water;
a circle of old waning friends;
a chance to gaze upon the perfect,
exquisite body of Night.

And when you feel a little lonely,
I'll be here in some ancient book;
waiting for you to look up, and open your palms;
my words, a white-hot burning
across the dark torso of time.

Tiny Courtships

I have lost my rush;
hurry sinking into the sand
like water.

I have watched the sun set
for three weeks; let myself
be rescued by handsome men.

Father once told me
chivalry was actually a gift
women give to *men*—
letting men use their God-given strengths
of muscle and protection.

He said it honours a man
when you wait for him,
when you let him carry your load.

For 43 years, my mother gently stood
by the door for him,
let him pull her chair at the table,

let him carry the awkward, the heavy,
let him rush fist-first into every volatile situation
while she stood back
to enter, to sit, to take, to nurse.

I have come back to the sea
after the plunging of youth,
to remember the sweet slowing—

the physical sensations
of lighting candles, and turning records,
and conversation;

the tiny courtships of women and men
like the pull and pulse of waves;

my hand wrapped tight in his;
my pockets full of shells.

Tequila Poetry Form
(2-2-4-3)

i think
maybe
i just might be
hung-over

Sin

Who
could deny
themselves
the Muse
who comes,
singing;

violets
in her hair.

Seasons

Maybe we are misinterpreting the Seasons.

Maybe a *good* Summer, to Summer,
is one where he rips open his shirt,
buttons flinging down across
his dark equator of ribs,
like meteors;
earth scalded by his gilded chest.

Maybe that's the goal of Summer—
all his strength wielded in solar testosterone
to make us crack and beg;
to singe the flesh down to bones.

And maybe a *good* Winter, to Winter,
is total white ice annihilation—
reaching her scissor-sharp toes
down into the mud of the Gulf,
the fish, flash-frozen mid swim.

Maybe it's their offspring we should
be wooing to stay longer—
chatty Spring, with her green highlights
and perky new breasts,

and her gay brother, Fall,
in his pumpkin turtleneck.
Fall, the sensitive poet
contemplating longer nights;
sharpened turkey quills in hand;

leaves falling as he shakes
his golden hair from his eyes.

God Bless America

She said *everything* was better
in *her* country,
especially the food—
the eggs, for example.

In America, she said,
you eat unfertilized eggs,
but in *her* country,

they prefer the fertilized ones;
the crunch of tiny bones.

God in the Bathtub

God Says Yes to Me
— Kaylin Haught

Sometimes when I light candles,
God steps into the room, an aged
whiskey in one hand, tight cigar in the other.
Sometimes He joins me in the bath,

stretching His handsome, narrow feet
and long toes out next to mine.
Last night, I asked how He could be
in my tub *and* all over the world

at the same time. He said that was
the Holy Ghost thing—covering
the whole earth in the same moment
like a veil of smoke.

I asked if He created humans because
He was lonely. "Beauty," He answered
with some wise bath pearl Proverb,
"was *always* meant to be shared."

After a while in the silence and the warmth
I asked if *after* He made the earth and the beasts
and mankind, if He *still* ever got lonely. He paused
for a moment, like my husband used to do,

using the long drag of tobacco to articulate
heavy thoughts. "Yea," He said, leaning
back, closing those great grey eyes,
"*that* kind of lonely is the worst."

Twelve Stitches

Even the balsamic taste of caprese
can take me back to that day before Easter,
my brother and I colouring eggs;

Dad's temper flaring in the next room;
summoning Jesus with every failed
attempt of engine restoration.

Ah . . . *the holidays*, those holy days of
togetherness, rushing to the hospital from
flying steel parts; my brother's stigmata—

blood on his hands; his head;
one stitch for every year of his life.
And my father at the wheel,

still calling out to the Lord,
blessings on the blood, the traffic;
the Craftsman tools.

Reference Material

He bought the book for its inscription
at the re-sell store, the handwritten note
from one lover to the other, declaring
eternal devotion: *In your quiet moments,*
may you always remember our love.

At home he placed it on the shelf,
next to the dictionary, thesaurus,
and the book about Pompeii, where
on page 36, a photo is earmarked—
a skeleton trapped in a house

on August 24, '79;
with only hours to live, suffocating
from the falling Vesuvius ash, he had
scratched into the beautifully frescoed wall:
Nothing in this world can endure forever.

Shameless Love Poem

You, my love, are the perfect evening,
arms outstretched to balance

the tumbling sun in one hand,
the cool moon in the other;

you, the giver of light to the world.
And when you come home,

your brow ridged with work,
iridescence spins about your face,

stardust lingers in the crease of your wrists,
the crescent beds beneath your nails.

And still you reach for me,
enough shimmer left

to light the doorway, the room,
the dark space between my lips.

My Moment of America

for my brother, General Richard Martin

Years before, he swore he'd never eject,
said the rigors of losing a 14 billion dollar
airplane could outweigh survival.
But he changed his mind

300 feet off the ground,
his F-16 nose-diving into
the Turkish desert,
and pulled that lever—

a rocket beneath his seat;
his country in his heart;
God in his parachute,
and walked away.

That was *my* moment of America,
to realize flesh and blood—
my flesh and blood—would gladly
give his life; willingly stand before

the snarl of death. . . . And each time I hear
that "Star-Spangled Banner" play,
I think of him there,
his grin beckoning *Come and Take It*;

behind him, the rocket's red glare.

veronica

> *a movement bullfighters do with their red capes to encourage*
> *a charging bull. It's taken from St. Veronica, who is always*
> *shown holding a veil in two hands like a matador's cape. The*
> *myth is that a woman named Veronica wiped Jesus' face on*
> *her veil, and that veil forever held His image. It's believed now,*
> *that an unknown woman wiped His face, and St. Veronica*
> *never existed — the vision on the veil was called **ver** (true) **icon***
> *(image) — **veronica**. Stories and time filled in the gaps.*

Because I could not spend the day with you,
I slipped away to this safe café—
not too public; not too intimate,
and eavesdropped on the conversations around me,

comforted by female chatter;
the tink of spoons to dishes;
kitchen noises.

Come gather the women;
the softened bodies;
the graying hair; the books, the quiche;
a red napkin in each lap.

It's an interesting thing—
our lives with men;
our lives without men.

Because I could not spend the day with you,
these places become arenas
of cool, feminine moons
who realize men are like the sun—

bright bulls of light
who pace the floors, and fade the chairs;
who burst through our lives
all heat and horn,

and we advance and tend,
evade and retreat—
and shimmy the red capes of our skirts
to woo them from their *querencia*[*] . . .

Come gather the men—
the hungry, the fearless, the wounded.

"Toro, Toro" tease the rounded women.
Into the myth, burn the men.

---

*querencia—area of the ring chosen by the bull where it feels secure

Her Night Eyes

written to be read out loud by Morgan Freeman

One hour after sunset, I paced
while she dressed
and powdered her face,
and darkened the abyss
of her eyes;

then gasped as I saw her
piercing the threshold of my earth,
hand on hip,
posing for the cameras
of my eyes;

and the black anger scatted back
to my shadow,
impatience vanished like fog from
the spell of her,

the blossom,
damp,
cool
smell of her.

Oh you, the Moon
of my night,
take my skin; let's slip
a little sin in our sway;

you who *electrify* the stars
of the night;
let us heed the primal pull
let's *go forth and multiply.*

A Little Flower

"Just living is not enough," said the Butterfly, "one must have sunshine, freedom, and a little flower."
        — Hans Christian Anderson

Sunbathing beneath the pear tree,
her lime green leaves flirting
in front of jealous oaks,
she called me outside;
the early warmth, an invitation
to shed my fleece and jeans and socks
down to a camisole and yellow panties;
white flowers falling on my skin
like scented spring snow.

I was told not to plant her—
her life, frail and fast;
but *she* is the brazen one—
the first bud, first blossom,
first plaything of the wind,
first desire of young bees;
laughing as winter beats his chest;
the girl with the longest summer;
her ruffling skirts of green.

Cooking with the Texas Poets Laureate
(Texas Review Press)

Jell-O Healing

Four days without food
leads to a feast of Jell-O—
bright red strawberry happiness.

I like how it forms to the cup,
the way my spoon curves out its own shape.
I feel it slide the long driveway into the stomach—
the cool opening of the belly.

I do not know how God merges everything in our life;
every little detail of our magnificent body;
but some wee stomach guard ushered it right in
to be divvied up in little straw baskets
and delivered—to the muscles,
to the blood; to the heart.

My daughter said her vegetarian friends
won't eat Jell-O—
says they're made from horse hooves . . .
and I smile at the thought of all those hooves—
all those cleft cuticles
ground up and stomping through my body;

the rage of Earth and Grass and Sun;
glorious snorting, steaming steeds;
those four perfect legs;
that broken-out gallop
that unsaddled strength.

Paris as I See It

for Elise Pierce

She said what she loves about Paris
are *the possibilities*;
the way sunrise smells
like warm croissants,

and midnight smells like pizza.
How morning stirs the colours in the Seine,
and people prefer formal grammar,
yet *french* in full view on the Metro;

how apartments are ranked
Haussmann and postwar;
how dogs are everywhere
but children rarely seen;

how current events take second
to pure butter, roasted chicken
and chocolate crepes;
how champagne comes before the wine;

and the locals smile as she butchers
the language, because that's *exactly*
how they like it—rich and tough,
but *perfect* with a nice bottle of red.

Damn Dishes

Give me
lime and butter and salt and chicken
and I will make you a happy man.

Just try walking into a house
with a bird in the oven
and *not* fall in love

Yes, your stomach says,
this could be your life—
this woman could feed you;
could make magic from produce
and frozen chicken thighs

Later, after sex,
you walk out to bones and dirty dishes
and soft annoyance,
who's gonna clean up this mess?

This, sir, is why
you will always be
a single man

What Clings to the Back
of the Spoon

There was no mention
of spareribs
or chicken-fried steak
and gravy . . .
but then, *that* was a lesson
we could have easily taught *them*.

But when I asked
about *their* favourite food,
they spoke of
growing up in England
with Mum's onion soup,
and Scotch eggs,
and cheese and pickle sandwiches.
Their eyes clouded,
and they had to clear their throats
to get back to the day's lesson
about foie gras and mirepoix,
and how you know the crème is *perfect*:
when it clings
to the stirring spoon.

And I realized then,
how much alike we all were
in that little French Cookery,
a spoon in every hand,
because what it all boils down to,
no matter where you're from,
is the way Mum smiled and said your name
as she called you in
to set the table for supper.

Music Box Lunch

This is why we travel this way—

with a blanket and ice chest,
and a map rolled in King Ranch

leather—for these endless acres
just beyond the Brazos, joyfully
trespassing in the round shade

of hay bales, sharing cold chicken and plums
and brownies. Let the traffic have its
fast food, rushing to destinations,

ours has always been about the road—
the line; the curve; hands clasped
between the seats—our love,

devouring time like twigs in a fire . . .
There is a rhythm here—a lid, lifted
off a box of magic—music wound

by the circling black wings above us;
hay bales placed like perfectly scored
pins; the comb of the wind, plucking

each golden ball—a song of time
that's meant to be opened;
a song of the moment—

when it's all about the dappling sun,
the smell of the river, and
a thousand miles of road yet to come.

Farewell to a Dear Friend and Poetry Patriarch, Dr. Paul Ruffin, Founder of the Texas Review Press

All it took with Paul Ruffin was one meeting,
one face-to-face encounter,
and you would always remember him. Always.
That is how it is with legends.
Life is lived on their terms—with a frying pan and a six-shooter;
a good pair of boots, strong coffee, and stronger whiskey.
As many will completely understand, he asked for my work,
and I offered it with two palms turned upward in gratitude.
He knew his business. He passed it forward.
He had no time, and much less desire, for mediocrity.
He was deeply respected.
He was deeply loved.
And it is this Love that we carry with us into the next life.
Who he was lifted us all,
and will continue to lift the next seven generations.
It was my great honor in this life to call him friend.

~ karla k. morton